Table of Contents

DISCLAIMER

As a matter of legality, please know that this book is not intended to diagnose, treat, or cure any part of infertility or any other disease that you may be experiencing. This book is in no way meant to substitute consulting with your physician.

Please also know that you will not find any special diets and get-pregnant-quick tricks because these things simply don't exist, and there won't be any pointing fingers or commands on what to do or not to do because, as part of an infertility community, those things are not in our genetic makeup.

What will you find? You will find useful information regarding infertility, whether a new or seasoned traveler, that will help you navigate your own journey. There are plenty of statistics, tips, real-life examples, and more that not only validate the things you're going through, but that can be used for inspiration while you cope.

I, Frances Hoelsema, as well as the many other women that contributed to this content, want nothing more than for you to find comfort in knowing you're not crazy, you're not alone, and there is always hope.

Also, as a side note, please know that this book will contain some religious references, including multiple Bible verses. If this is not your type of thing, please feel free to bypass those sections, or perhaps pass on this book all together. I, in no way, want to offend anyone so please proceed in the way that best suits your comfortability.

Part One

***

First Things First

1

Getting Pregnant Is NOT Easy

Let's travel back in time together to when you were in elementary school. This tends to be the time when the public education system starts sex ed. I don't know about you, but I remember my experience clearly. It was a one-night affair in the fifth grade during the middle of the school year. The boys went into a room with their parent(s) as well as a male teacher. The girls were put into a separate room with their parent(s) as well as a female teacher. Then came the video.

All of us girls sat quietly as we watched what would happen with our bodies in the coming years. And then at the end of the video was a short clip on what the boys would be experiencing. I remember many of the girls thinking it was so unfair the things we have to go through. The boys definitely got the easy end of the bargain when it came to our changing bodies. Regardless, when the video ended, there was a short time for questions and that was it.

In the sixth through eighth grades, there was always a small segment carved out of the school year where, in science class, we would delve deeper into the human body. This time the teachers dared to allow both the girls and boys to stay in the same class together, and let me be the first to say that there was a fair share of giggles and pointing going on. This only intensified when the subject of how babies were created was introduced. Again, it's not like we went deep into the subject matter. Everything was basically treated like a hot potato. The teachers wanted to get rid of the information as quickly as possible, and most, if not all, of the students wanted this part of the school day to be over with, like, yesterday.

I'm not sure if your experience matches mine or if it's far from it, but I think it would be safe to say that during this time in our lives, having babies was not on our radar. Yes, many of us women had this general sense that we knew that when we grew up we wanted to be married and have children. Many of us would even play "house" where we acted out the role of mother. But that was the extent of our thinking. And, yes, we saw babies, heard about how they were created, etc., but never once did we give thought to creating one ourselves or the ups and downs that go along with that process. At this stage, we were all just hoping that nothing embarrassing would happen, like our period showing up without warning and without any protection.

Fast forward just a tad to high school. Sex education begins to take a much bigger role in the classroom. This time it's not so much about our bodies and the way they will change because, honestly, at this point we've all gone through the changes or are at least in the midst of them. High school is the time to start really talking about what we can do with these girl and boy body parts. In other words, sex.

At this point sex is not just an act that's used to create a baby, as we learned in the previous years. Sex is now an activity couples do because they get a lot of enjoyment out of it. Sex is something fun. And now that we're at an age where our hormones are raging and the idea of finding a mate to procreate with is getting more and more attractive, it's also something that even the very students in the classroom learning about it are doing.

Throughout our high school careers, we're taught that sex equals one or two things. It could lead to an STD or it could lead to pregnancy. So, a lot of focus in the public education system is on safe sex. We're warned to use a condom if we're going to have sex because that should protect you from anything "bad" that could happen.

Again, I'm not sure what your experience was. Your school may or may not have done a better job with sex ed. I also do not know what is taught or how it's taught in schools around the nation today. But I do feel there are a lot of truths from what I went through. I do think there is a heavy focus on sex = babies, which no one can disagree on. And while I do believe that sex education is extremely important, I also feel that it misses the mark. There needs to be a bit of a touch of reality mixed in.

Raise your hand if you grew up thinking infertility could be a problem. Is infertility something that you studied or were told could happen? I certainly had no clue. It was ingrained in my mind that when I did want to have kids, I just had to have sex and I'd be able to get pregnant.

I knew there was such a thing as adoption, but I thought couples only did that because they wanted to and not because they needed to. And I also had one aunt that, through the grapevine, I heard had a hard time getting pregnant. But never in a million years did I think having a difficult time getting pregnant was something that happened on a pretty regular basis.

Never did I think it would happen to me.

Sex Doesn't Always Equal Babies

The reality of fertility is that it might take a while to actually get pregnant. Did you know that in any given month, a healthy woman between the ages of 20 and 25 only has a 25% chance of conceiving? That means that there is a 75% chance that she won't. Even in a young, healthy woman, the odds are against you.

If that wasn't bad enough, the older you get, the worse your chances. Those 25 to 30 have only a 20% chance of getting pregnant. Those 30 to 35 have only a 15% chance. If you're 35 to 40, you only have a 10% chance, and so on and so on. Basically, the older you get, the chances of conceiving decreases. Also, as you age, the probability of producing abnormal eggs and miscarrying increases. And this is all for a "healthy" woman. Imagine adding in any kind of "issue" and you're left with far worse statistics. If you would like to see these statistics and more, Our Baby Namer, a website dedicated mostly to baby names, does a good job laying out the facts.

As if conceiving wasn't tough enough, what about staying pregnant? I mean, just look at these astonishing statistics. An article on Verywell, a reliable source for hundreds of health and wellness topics, shared a study that showed as much as 22% of conceptions end in failed implantations. This means you could have very well conceived, but never knew it because your period came anyway.

For those who have the great experience of an implantation sticking and then seeing a positive on a pregnancy test, Verywell shares that they still have a 15% to 20% chance of miscarrying. Most of those who do will do so in the first trimester when all of the crucial fetal development is taking place. But about 3% to 4% still have the chance of doing so beyond that critical time. Then after 20 weeks, a woman still has a 1 in 160 chance their pregnancy will end in a stillbirth.

The Miracle of Life

Back in 2001, PBS aired a documentary called Life's Greatest Miracle. If you go to their website, which I have listed in the back of this book, you can learn more about it as well as order a DVD of the program. It does a phenomenal job sharing what a miracle life really is. The website also has the full transcript should you be interested in reading through the show's entirety. Here are a few of the main points:

- A baby, once only one single cell, "comprises of one hundred trillion cells with hundreds of different kinds of tissues and dozens of organs, including a brain that allows it to do amazing things." Keep in mind that should anything happen during this process, the pregnancy will result in death of the baby or a life-long deformity.

- A man produces new sperm every single day where as a woman is born with all the eggs she'll ever get. "Within a couple months, a woman creates several million eggs. And then the eggs begin to die. By the age of 31, there may be only a few thousand left." Thus, the reason age is extremely important when it comes to fertility. The younger a woman, the more eggs she will have, as well as the better the quality of those eggs.

- "The egg has everything it needs to start a new life except DNA from a sperm." Once released from the ovary, it will die if not fertilized within a few hours. So, timing has to be everything, right?

- A man releases approximately 300 million sperm when he orgasms. But because the vagina is so acidic, they have to either "escape or die". So, they swim! Some of them anyway. "Even in a healthy man, 60% of the sperm are less than perfect." If you're a sperm that's less than perfect, you're done for. Sounds like you still have a good chance of getting pregnant, though, right? Let's continue on.

- Sperm face many challenges. The cervix is usually "locked shut", and those that make it inside the uterus are still roughly "six inches away from their goal". That may not seem far, but to sperm it's about a two-day journey. If they're lucky enough to get to the fallopian tube, a mature egg needs to be there for anything to possibly happen.

- Say a mature egg is making its way through the fallopian tube. It's still "heavily chaperoned by support cells, and those chaperones are very picky." This means only a handful of the sperm that have made it so far are given a chance to get in.

· If a sperm is lucky to break its way in, their chances of creating a viable embryo are still not great. "It's estimated that more than 50% of all fertilized eggs fail to develop." Those that do start to develop "must complete just the right number of cell divisions before they arrive in the uterus about five days after fertilization". If you haven't noticed already, there is a lot of work that goes into making a baby.

· When an egg attaches to the wall of the uterus, the mother's own immune system "could attack" it because it sees the fertilized egg as a "foreign invader". Of course, if our bodies would listen to what we wanted, this wouldn't be the case. But that's obviously not reality. And, of course, if our bodies don't attack, we'll find out we're pregnant.

· "Inside the womb, the first few weeks are the most dramatic." This is when cells keep multiplying and organs develop. This would also be the time a miscarriage is most likely to happen due to something going wrong in all the multiplications.

The program goes on to reveal more on fetal development and the miracle of birth that are just fascinating. Since that's not what this book is about, though, we'll just stop here.

What you can see from this documentary is that everything has to align perfectly in order for conception to take place, implantation to be successful, and development to be healthy and normal. Our man's sperm has to be active and correctly formed, our eggs need to be matured and released, our uterus needs to be a hospitable environment, and all of our hormones need to do their job in sustaining a fetus. And these are just naming a few of the important parts involved with getting pregnant. We can't just go through a mental check list and assume it'll all work out. Can you imagine if that were true?

Ovulating? Check!

Had sex? Check!

Boom! Two weeks later and you get a positive pregnancy test!

Then 9 months later out pops your bundle of joy!

Seriously, ladies, if it were that easy, not only would we have a population problem, but books like this wouldn't need to be around.

What Does This All Mean?

If you're like me, these facts will seem pretty amazing yet highly discouraging. However, in a weird way, they can also provide the slightest bit of comfort in my opinion. After all, if you're going through a tough time trying to conceive, like I once did, the odds were never in our favor to begin with. And that's the same across the board for every single woman, infertility or no infertility. So, this means it's not like it was some easy feat that you should kick yourself for because you weren't able to accomplish it. It's not something that is technically your fault. It's not something you can even completely control. This is simply just the way life and our bodies were designed.

Now I know it seems like every time you turn to your right or to your left you see another pregnant woman. It's those women that make conceiving appear easy, but the statistics don't lie. The truth is, conceiving and carrying a baby to full term is nothing short of a miracle. No wonder we are dealing with conception issues. It's truly hard.

Unfortunately for many of us, due to one reason or another, it's even harder.

2

What Infertility Really Is

Have you ever heard of RESOLVE? If you haven't, now is the time to learn. I can't say enough good things about this organization. RESOLVE: The National Infertility Association was established in 1974 and exists to provide resources to people, such as yourself, who are going through infertility. RESOLVE's website has so many great sources to check out from basic information, to support groups, to finding professional options. In a sense, it's your one-stop shop for anything and everything infertility related. Should you like to check the website out, which I highly recommend you do, I have it listed in the back of this book.

RESOLVE provides this definition of infertility: "the inability to conceive or carry a pregnancy to term after 12 months of trying to conceive." Simply put, if you and your partner have been trying for a baby for at least a year and have yet to get or stay pregnant, you would be diagnosed as suffering from infertility.

Within infertility there are two sub-groups, all depending on when the infertility is taking place. Those suffering from primary infertility are those that have never had the opportunity to get pregnant, or if they have, they've never been able to carry the pregnancy to full term; the woman either miscarries or has a stillbirth. Secondary infertility, on the other hand, are those who have at least one biological child that was conceived without medical help, but now, for one reason or another, are not able to get pregnant again and/or carry the pregnancy to full term.

There are also four different kinds of infertility, all depending on who is the contributor to the disease. Female infertility, where the female is the only one with an "issue", makes up about 30% of couples going through infertility. You might find this surprising, but male infertility, where the male is the only one with an "issue", also makes up 30% of the total number of couples going through infertility. 10% of infertility is caused by a combination of problems in both the female and male.

And the other 20%? Well, that type of infertility is known as unexplained, meaning no one has a clue as to why you aren't conceiving. All forms of infertility suck, but unexplained has got to be one of the worst because there's essentially no reason as to why you aren't conceiving, and there's not a single "issue" you can work on to help you conceive.

This is infertility in a nutshell, so to speak. If someone were to ask you for a definition and this information was what you were to give them, you'd pass the test with flying colors. But what about a little extra credit? I mean, we all know that infertility is more than this. Way, way more than something that could be put in a standard textbook.

Beyond the Science of Medicine

Beyond what the doctors will tell you, those actually experiencing infertility can put a better definition on it. Let's examine some of them and see if you agree.

- **Infertility is a silent disease.** What do I mean by this? Well, if one in eight couples, that's 12.5%, are struggling with infertility according to RESOLVE's website, why is it not something we hear more about? Maybe it's because of some of the feelings that we deal with as we make our way on this journey like feeling inferior, or less of a woman, or even ashamed. I'm not really sure, but whatever the reason, people just generally don't speak about the struggles they're facing in regard to conceiving.

    Take part of my story as an example. I mentioned before that I had this aunt who I heard about that struggled to get pregnant, but I never heard of anyone else going through infertility or having a miscarriage before. Boy did that all change when I had my own miscarriage. It was like the floodgates had been opened! All of the sudden many women approached me with their own miscarriage story and/or their own personal struggle to getting pregnant. I was shocked; I seriously had no clue! I went from feeling extremely out of place and even abnormal to feeling almost "common" in a matter of a heartbeat. Those initial feelings could have been totally avoided had I heard others speaking about it before.

    But, of course, I understand why you wouldn't just bring it up to someone, though. After all, infertility doesn't exactly seem like the kind of topic that screams "fascinating", or "interesting", or even "must share"! There's got to be some middle ground, though, right? Maybe, maybe not. Either way, as it stands now, it's considered a silent disease.

· **Infertility is an invisible disease.** Unless you have this amazing sixth sense on being able to tell if someone is infertile or not, I'd say it's pretty invisible. No one can tell if someone else is going through infertility. Sure, there are families who have children that are racially different. It's easy to think that those couples must have had a hard time getting pregnant so they adopted. But there's no way to know with 100% certainty that, that is the case.

There are also couples that have been married for eons of years that have no children at all. A lot of people might conclude it's because they couldn't get pregnant. While that is a possibility, there is, again, no way to know for sure just by looking at them.

So, in a nutshell, you can't tell if someone else is going through infertility just by looking at them, and no one can tell you're going through infertility just by looking at you. Which, I might add, probably adds to the fact no one talks about it because who in their right mind just walks up to someone and blatantly asks, "Hey, are you having a tough time getting pregnant?"

· **Infertility is the inability to do what God clearly asks us to do.** Right in the very first chapter of the Bible, God instructs the male and female he created to, "Be fruitful and multiply. Fill the earth and govern it" (Genesis 1:28).

And this command was not just for Adam and Eve. In Genesis 9:1 where God blessed Noah and his sons, He said, "Now be fruitful and multiply, and repopulate the earth."

Take a look at this Bible passage. "Did the Lord make you one with your wife? In body and spirit, you are His. And what does He want? Godly children from your union" (Malachi 2:15).

God wants us and commands us to have children. Obviously, you want to and are trying to obey, but your infertility, being what it is, is getting in the way.

· **Infertility is hell on earth.** Those in the deepest, darkest parts of their journey will be able to agree with this one. Infertility produces so much pain and despair. Add on top of it the distance you feel from God and you've basically got yourself a hell on earth.

· **Infertility is many things.** One woman described infertility in this way: "Infertility is gut-wrenching, heartbreaking, faith testing, marriage testing, a grace-filled rollercoaster of hope and despair; a myriad of emotions and experiences. My greatest test of faith that has brought me face to face with my own deficiencies and failures, yet has also brought me face to face with a loving God who knows exactly where I am and why He trusted me to walk this lonely, barren way. It's my greatest strength now because it's taught me compassion and empathy for the hurting, and yet it's also my greatest weakness. I can never define my infertility by one word. It's a depth of emotions and time that varies on any given day or moment. Right now, today, infertility means battle weary to me. I'm tired of it all."

When I saw that definition, I immediately asked if I could use it for this book because it is the epitome of what anyone's infertility journey looks like. It's not just one thing or another. It's so many things on so many levels, and each day is usually vastly different from the next. Some days you'll experience all of it, while other days it might just be a thing or two. The woman who said this could not have pinned the tail on the donkey more accurately.

· **Infertility is undefinable.** I know that I just got done saying that infertility is so many different things. I'm not reneging on that statement one bit. However, I truly feel it can be all those things, yet undefinable. There are days where you just can't put a word on what's going on. There are times where you just can't explain what you're going through if someone were to ask. I feel like infertility is really in a league of its own where you can't even begin to help someone else understand it. There's just no words for it. It just is what it is.

The Perfect Storm

There are probably many things you could add to this list on defining infertility. Some days you might be able to clearly resonate with a few of these statements, and I'm sure there will be days where you completely disagree with some while the others look more accurate. One thing can be agreed upon for sure, though, and that is that infertility is a huge problem with many sufferers and so few supporters. Add in the fact that there is no 100% proven cure that works for every single couple, I'd say infertility is truly the perfect storm. No wonder a lot of woman (men, too) struggle with trying to figure out how to cope with it and through it.

I'm willing to bet that you are reading this book because you are struggling with infertility. That being said, I first want to say that I'm sorry you have this storm welling up within you. I also want to say that I'm humbly grateful that you took a chance on reading this book. In the pages to follow, I'm going to fill you in on what you can expect during this tough journey, as well as give you some pointers on how to be inspired while you wait. Depending on how long you've suffered, some of this information may be old news to you, but I hope you'll still gain some new perspectives and walk away from this book with a fresh step towards seeing your way through this part in your life.

So, without further ado, let's start with you!

Part Two

***

What to Expect for Yourself

3

Say What?

I'm going to let you in on a little secret. If you haven't figured it out by now, those suffering with infertility have their own little club. In fact, one woman phrased it this way: "Infertility is a club you never wanted to join, and also a club you'll never leave. Only we know the secret handshake and the rest of the world will never understand." Having said that, let me be the first to welcome you in! Yes, I know you'd rather not be here, though.

Expect to Learn Some New Lingo

As part of this club, the secret handshake referred to means many things. One of them is that you will get a new language to call your very own! It's the type of language that only you and your fellow infertility peers will get. Doctors and other specialists will know the more professional ones, but otherwise it's just you and the rest of the club.

If you're just starting your infertility journey, you may not know some of these terms yet so I am going to list some of the more common ones below. Those of you who have been around for a long time will probably want to breeze through these because it's something you probably already know.

Also, to make it easy, I have divided the terms into two groups. The first list will be the more professional words that you will learn to use amongst "average" people (people you actually see on a day-to-day basis as opposed to online), as well as your doctor or any other specialists you are seeing. I will label these "medical terminology".

The second set of words I'm going to label as "urban dictionary". Just like the real Urban Dictionary you can find online, this list of words consists of slang terms, made-up phrases, and lots and lots of acronyms. These words you will commonly use just online within support groups because it's so much easier to type out the shortened version of something than the full-length one. If you were to begin to use some of these words in your everyday vocabulary, though, people will either not understand or think you're referring to something completely different.

Take for example the two-letter word PG. If you were to type this out to your infertility friends, they're going to know you're talking about the word pregnant. However, if you were to say PG to the "average" person, they're going to think you're referring to some kind of rating.

Another example is the two-letter word AF. I'm not going to say what your "average" people will think you're saying as it's not a clean phrase. But your infertility peers are going to know you're just talking about your period.

Finally, these lists will be separated because even if a doctor or other "average" person did understand what you were saying, you probably wouldn't come out and say, "My last AF was three weeks ago." We all know that you would just say menstrual cycle or period.

Medical Terminology

There are a lot of good sources online that do an excellent job with listing some infertility terms and their meanings. I went with an article I found on WebMD because, not only is WebMD highly regarded and professional, I thought everything was laid out nicely and can be easily understood. What I have listed here is by no means the complete dictionary of all fertility/infertility-related terms. I am only listing the more common ones that you'd be more likely to encounter.

- **Amenorrhea** – a condition in which a woman doesn't have menstrual periods. As a side note, there is primary and secondary amenorrhea. Primary is when a woman hasn't menstruated before 16 years of age. Secondary is when a woman has regularly menstruated, but then due to one reason or another, they have stopped.

- **Anovulation** – a condition in which a woman doesn't ovulate or ovulates rarely.

- **Assisted Reproduction Technology (ART)** – the general term for infertility procedures (involving both egg and sperm) such as IVF, GIFT, ZIFT, and ICSI.

- **Basal Body Temperature (BBT)** – a temperature reading that can be used to chart ovulation when taken every day.

· **Cervical Mucus** – mucus produced by the cervix that increases in quantity as ovulation approaches.

· Clomid – a fertility drug given to women to stimulate ovulation.

· Endometriosis – a painful condition in which tissue from the lining of the uterus (the endometrium) grows outside of the uterus.

· Follicle Stimulating Hormone **(FSH)** – a hormone produced in the pituitary gland that causes cells in the ovaries to grow.

· **Gamete Intrafallopian Transfer (GIFT)** – an assisted reproductive technique that involves removing sperm and eggs, mixing them together, and placing them into the fallopian tubes.

· Human Chorionic Gonadotropin **(HCG)** – a hormone that can be used to trigger ovulation.

· **Hysterosalpingogram (HSG)** – an X-ray which involves injecting dye through the cervix into the uterus to determine if the fallopian tubes are open and the uterine cavity is normal.

· **Intracytoplasmic Sperm Injection (ICSI)** – a procedure in which sperm and eggs are retrieved. A single sperm is then injected directly into an egg and then the fertilized egg is implanted into the woman's uterus.

· **Intrauterine Insemination (IUI)** – an artificial insemination technique in which sperm are put directly into a woman's uterus at the time she is ovulating.

· In Vitro Fertilization **(IVF)** – an assisted reproductive technique that involves removing sperm and eggs, fertilizing them in a laboratory, and then placing a fertilized egg in the uterus.

· Luteinizing Hormone – a hormone that triggers ovulation.

· **Luteal Phase** – the second half of the menstrual cycle.

· **Morphology** – the size and shape of sperm.

· **Motility** – the ability of sperm to move by themselves.

· **Ovulation** – when the ovaries release a mature egg that is ready for fertilization.

- **Polycystic Ovary Syndrome (PCOS)** – a common hormonal condition in which an imbalance in the sex hormones may cause menstrual abnormalities, skin and hair changes, obesity, infertility, and other long-term health problems. The name comes from the multiple small cysts which line the ovaries of most women with the disorder.

- **Postcoital Test** – a standard fertility test in which a sample of cervical mucus is taken after intercourse to check the number and behavior of the sperm.

- **Semen Analysis** – a standard test of a man's semen to check the number and shape of his sperm and their motility.

- **Varicocele** – a varicose vein in the scrotum that may affect the quality and the production of sperm.

- **Zygote Intrafallopian Transfer (ZIFT)** – an assisted reproductive technique similar to IVF that involves removing sperm and eggs, combining them outside the body, and inserting fertilized eggs into the fallopian tubes.

Urban Dictionary

There's nothing wrong with the technical terms we just saw, but I think the list I am about to share is a little more fun. The following words are what really put infertility sufferers into their own club as I mentioned before. Some are really creative, and all of them make explaining things so much easier.

If you'd like to see a more complete list, please check out RESOLVE's website. They do a phenomenal job listing out acronyms you might come across. Here, however, are some of the most common:

- **2WW/TWW** – two-week wait – referring to the time between ovulation and your period/positive pregnancy test.

- **AF** – aunt flow – referring to your period.

- **AI** – artificial insemination – the procedure of putting sperm into the uterus.

· **BD** – baby dance – in other words, sex.

· **BFN/BFP** – big fat negative/big fat positive – referring to the result of a pregnancy test.

· **B/W** – bloodwork – refers to bloodwork done associated with infertility.

· **CB** – cycle buddy – those that started their periods the same day as you and who will go through the entire cycle with you.

· **CD** – cycle day – refers to what day of your cycle you are on.

· **CP** – cervical position – refers to if your cervix is high or low.

· **CM** – cervical mucus – refers to the consistency of the mucus found near the cervix.

· **DH** – dear husband – refers to your mate.

· **DPO** – days past ovulation – refers to how many days you are after you've ovulated.

· **ENDO** – endometriosis – just a shorter (and easier, in my opinion) way of referring to this health problem.

· **HPT** – home pregnancy test – that one might be a no-brainer.

· **LMP** – last menstrual period – the date when your last period started.

· **MC** – miscarriage – just a shorter way of referring to the loss of a baby before 20 weeks.

· **MF** – male factor – refers to the man having the "issue" in your journey.

· **O** – ovulation – that's an easy acronym.

· **OPT** – ovulation predictor test – possibly another no-brainer.

· **PG** – pregnant – a shortened way to say pregnant.

· **POAS** – peeing on a stick – refers to taking a test, either ovulation or pregnancy.

· **RE** – reproductive endocrinologist – a handy acronym so you don't have to spell those two big words out.

· **SA** – semen analysis – refers to the test men take to determine the sperm count and motility.

· **TTC** – trying to conceive – that's what you're currently doing.

See, weren't those a little more fun? Like I said before, there's a lot more where those came from. I want to encourage you, again, to check out RESOLVE. They are just a really handy resource for anything surrounding infertility.

And, of course, if you still can't find what you're looking for, chances are if you do a search in Google or any other search engine, you should be able to figure it out. Living in today's day and age has a lot of perks because we have access to information at the drop of a hat.

If you're part of any online groups or forums, you could also ask the other participants and they'd be happy to help. One thing you'll quickly begin to realize about this club is that we are all really understanding, kind, and super helpful.

I know that it might seem like there are a lot of terms. It can really be mind boggling! However, these aren't as complicated as they seem. In no time, you'll be able to speak this new language with ease, especially if you have some online infertility friends.

If you're like me, once I started going through my infertility journey, I spent a good majority of my time with online infertility friends. I'm still friends with some of them today! So, because I was around that atmosphere a lot, and around doctors a lot, all of these terms became second in nature to me. They will for you, too!

Now let's shift to another type of "handshake" you can expect for yourself that only you and your fellow peers in the infertility club will ever understand.

4

Our Bodies Are Pretty Cool –
Well, Most of the Time

The human body is truly a work of art, isn't it? If you were to study everything that your body is made of and how it functions, you'd be left fascinated. I don't want to spend the time or space discussing all of our bodily systems, but let's pay particular attention to the reproductive system. After all, that's the part of a woman's body that was created to allow us to create and sustain life.

A female's reproductive system is made up of many parts, not only anatomically, but functionally as well. God designed our bodies to be equipped with a vaginal canal, cervix, uterus, fallopian tubes, and ovaries. Since this is something you learned back in elementary school, there's no need to discuss further the anatomy of a woman's body.

What I do think we should study for a brief moment is the functional aspect of our reproductive system. This is where, I think, we can look at our bodies and say they are pretty cool. Just think about your monthly cycle. God made it so that your body gears up and winds down every month, assuming you're not pregnant. If you were to be pregnant, your body will stay geared up until the pregnancy is over. WebMD lays it out so that it's super simple to understand, but here are the basics.

Towards the beginning of your cycle, your body releases follicle stimulating hormones and luteinizing hormones so that your body can stimulate growth of about 15 to 20 eggs and get them ready to be released. A third hormone that is important during this time, estrogen, is what will allow usually a single egg to mature. The most mature egg is what gets released. If estrogen wasn't doing its part, women could end up with 15 to 20 eggs released at a single time. If all of them were fertilized at the same time, I don't think anyone would want to think about what it would be like to have 15 to 20 babies growing inside our wombs at one time!

Once the mature egg is released, the finger-like ends of your fallopian tube snatch it up and bring it inside so that it can make its way to the uterus. This would be where sperm could reach it, should there be any available.

While this all takes place, the lining of your uterus begins to thicken with the aid of a fourth hormone called progesterone. You want to know where the progesterone comes from? The follicle that secreted the mature egg turns into corpus luteum. The corpus luteum is what gives off the progesterone. How cool is that?

Moving on, if the mature egg has been fertilized, it will try to attach to the lining of the uterus. If successful, you'll find out that you're pregnant in two weeks or less. If, however, the egg was not fertilized, the egg will disintegrate and the lining of the uterus will shed. In other words, you will get your period and start the cycle over again.

Now that this quick lesson is over with, let's look at some cool ways we can tell our bodies are changing throughout our cycles.

Expect to Get to Really Know Yourself

People, such as yourself, that are going through infertility tend to learn their bodies fairly well. This is because our bodies give off key indicators that point to our most fertile cycle days. The more fertile you are, the more chances you have of getting pregnant should you have sex. So, it only stands to reason that if getting pregnant is your end goal, you'll want to familiarize yourself with these signs. But as a fair warning, some of these you might feel uncomfortable performing. If that's the case, it's not like you will be hopeless. There are much less invasive, albeit one is more expensive, ways to determine your fertile window.

- **Cervical Position.** As your body goes through your monthly cycle, the positioning and feel of your cervix changes. At the beginning of your cycle the cervix is low, closed, firm, and usually dry. The closer you get to ovulation, your cervix rises, becomes softer, wetter, and begins to open up. The only way you'll be able to tell a difference is by testing it yourself. To do so, you will need to insert one or two clean fingers into the vagina and feel for the cervix. The key is to do this at the same time each day as there will be some slight changes throughout the day, depending on your activities. Like I mentioned before, reaching up inside of your vagina might give you the heebie-jeebies. It's okay if you don't want to check for this. You might also want to skip the next fertility indicator as well if that's the case.

· **Cervical Mucus.** This is another cool thing your body does as it gets closer to ovulation time. Right after your period ends, cervical mucus tends to be almost non-existent. It'll feel very dry down there. As the body ramps up, the dryness turns to stickiness and then to something more slippery. At the very height of your fertile window, the mucus given off by the cervix will almost be a raw egg-white consistency. This is to allow the sperm the ability to survive until it can meet the egg. And then after ovulation has already occurred, the mucus turns to a sticky state once again. To check for cervical mucus, you'll again want one or two clean fingers to reach up inside the vagina. It might as well be the same time you check for your cervical position, right? Anyway, when you pull your fingers out, evaluate the kind of mucus that is left on your fingers. Then finish up in the bathroom by thoroughly washing your hands! But, of course, you knew that already.

· **Mittelschmerz.** Do you know how to pronounce that? I really don't, but thankfully that's not needed to understand what this word actually is. Mittelschmerz is a German word that means "middle pain". It's basically a fancy way of saying a pain or tingly feeling you might feel on one side of your abdomen right around ovulation time. Unfortunately, not all women will experience this. However, I do think more women experience this without realizing it because they aren't paying close enough attention to their bodies.

· **Cycle Counting.** For those of you that have regular cycles, this will be a great tool to use in order to figure out when you'll ovulate and when you should get your next cycle. Ovulation usually takes place around 14 days before your period comes again. This derives the phrase two-week wait; it's the time you need to wait between ovulation and your period or positive pregnancy test. Again, for those that are regular, this would probably have to be the only tool you use. However, for women, such as myself, who have irregular cycles, cycle counting isn't as accurate. For me, my cycles were all over the place so I couldn't just depend on ovulating at a certain time. This is why I had to rely on other signs and symptoms to help me figure out what my body was up to.

· **Basel Body Temperature (BBT).** Even though this indicator isn't so much on when ovulation takes place, but on when it already happened, it's still one indicator I am in awe of. Let me explain why. Before ovulation, your body's internal temperature is roughly the same each morning. However, after you ovulate, your body's internal temperature is clearly higher and stays higher until your period comes or until after your pregnancy is over. Take my basal body temperatures for example. Before I ovulate, my internal temperature is usually upper 97s, like anywhere between 97.5 to 97.9 degrees. After I ovulate, my basal body temperatures are at least 98.4 degrees, but usually even higher. My first clue I had first gotten pregnant was because my basal body temperature stayed above 98.5 degrees for longer than 14 days. It's really awesome how God created our bodies to adjust like this. To take your basal body temperature, all you have to do is have an oral thermometer handy by your bedside. Then at the same time every morning, take your temperature and record it. When you see a clear shift in temps that last longer than three days, you will know that you have ovulated.

· **Cycle Charting.** Some people go all out and just do everything. They keep a nifty chart that showcases each day of their cycle, and what their daily temp was, their cervical position and mucus was, as well as any feelings they had for that day. They will indicate if they've had sex or not so they could look back and see if it's possible to be pregnant. They will also describe their periods to make sure it's normal for them, meaning regular, not too long, or painful. By looking at a complete chart, you can indicate your fertile window and when you finally ovulated. You'll also be able to see when your two-week wait is about up and if you should bother testing to see if you're pregnant.

All of this is why I mention that you'll get to really know your body. There are things that I never thought I'd ever do. And I mean never ever! However, I really wanted to figure out when the best time to have sex and get pregnant was, thus the need to get over my own shyness and dig into these fertile indicators. No pun intended. Well, maybe.

To bypass all of these things, you could just use OPKs (ovulation predictor kits). These are just like home pregnancy tests where you pee on a stick and the results will either indicate you're in your fertile window or not so much. While I have used these occasionally, and I do think they work to some extent, they are pricy. I also found that checking my own body worked better for me than these tests. And I understood myself better than some of the OPK results I have had.

All of the above information was from a website called Ovulation Calculator. It's an online preconception and pregnancy resource center that is worth checking out. Should you have any questions regarding any of these indicators, there is a lot more information on that site. I just skimmed the surface so to speak.

And like I said before, these are also some things that the "average" woman wouldn't understand either. She would have no need to check for her fertile window because she's never had a problem getting pregnant before. Some women will use the cycle counting method for family planning, but I think you could easily say that the "average" woman does not check basal body temperature, cervical position, and cervical mucus. Only those in the infertility club will do this, and only those in this club will understand why. How's that for a secret handshake?

Expect Occasional Body & Mind Tricking

As you become more familiar with your body, and especially if you chart, you may notice early on if you may be pregnant. WebMD lists a bunch of early pregnancy symptoms, including nausea, fatigue, sore breasts, frequent urination, and mood swings. By keeping track of your cycle days on a chart and the way you're feeling, you will have a better chance of knowing if you should bother taking a pregnancy test or not.

However, here comes the uncool part of our bodies. Remember when I said our bodies were cool most of the time? Well, here's the times it's not. No matter how good you get at knowing your body and predicting what's coming, your body can, and will, occasionally throw you off. And I swear it's just for kicks and giggles. Yes, your very own body that you've become so acquainted with recently will trick you from time to time. In other words, it will make you feel things and experience things that are completely false. Fake. A lie.

The medical term for this, as WebMD shares, is pseudocyesis, which is basically a fancy way of saying false pregnancy. As you guessed, it's when a woman (and even a man can have this, which is interesting) really thinks she's pregnant, but is clearly not. Doctors believe this is a completely psychological disorder because of the intense desire the woman has of getting pregnant. Get this. A woman can experience lack of menstruation, sore breasts, weight gain, and the myriad other pregnancy symptoms, but actually have no fetus growing inside of her. In rare cases, some women even end up in the ER because they think they are going through labor pains! Like I said, that's rare, but experiencing a small part of pseudocyesis if fairly common in my opinion. After all, I know that there were countless times as I charted that I would notice certain things and know beyond a shadow of a doubt that I just had to be pregnant. Of course, I wasn't because my period came anyway. But I can see how the body and mind work together just to fool us.

It's kind of like when you have a few symptoms of something so you go on Google or some other search engine to see what might be wrong with you. Obviously, you'll come across something deadly so you'll start to panic. Then you'll experience more of the symptoms of that deadly disease that you weren't experiencing before. The problem exacerbates so out of control that you're just dead certain that you do, in fact, have whatever disease it is you think you have. Has that happened to you? Please don't tell me I'm the only one! It's actually happened to me on more than one occasion. I really do need to stop playing doctor. Or at least stop letting Google play the doctor. But this is another prime example how the mind can trick us into thinking something, and then the body starts following suit.

On top of everything else we experience with our infertility, knowing deception can be the case, no wonder we're a basket case emotionally.

5

Not All Rollercoasters Are Fun

Does the idea of going to a theme park to ride the rollercoasters thrill you? It's not my cup of tea, but I know many people who enjoy them. When I think of rollercoasters, I think of either my head banging around or my stomach being stuck five stories high when I'm clearly near the ground. Many of you are able to look past those discomforts and ride them over and over again.

I can just picture you. You're waiting in line, and as you slowly inch your way closer to the ride, your excitement grows. You just can't wait to get on. Finally, it's your turn! You pick the perfect seat and get all buckled in, anticipating what's coming. As the rollercoaster begins its journey, it's first slow, but quickly gains speed. Here comes a hill! You start ascending, the coaster slowing down. It slows down so much that you are slightly nervous it might go backwards. Then for one brief moment you're on top of the world. You can see all around you for miles and you take in the beauty of creation.

Whoosh! Down you plummet to your death. As the rollercoaster races downward, your peaceful thoughts of all you've just seen left up on top of the hill, along with your stomach. However, you could care less! You scream and raise your arms to further enhance your experience. Your skin and hair is flying backwards, making you look unhuman at times. This process of going up a hill and back down a hill will probably repeat itself a few times before the ride is over.

Oh, and then there's at least one twist! Suddenly your body is jerked to the right or to the left as the rollercoaster cuts a corner so sharply that you think it'll jack knife. There's also a loop or two thrown in there, because, I mean, who doesn't like to be hanging upside down?

At last the ride is over. You catch your breath, smile to the person sitting next to you, and share with the world that you must do that again.

Fun is the word you might use to describe rollercoasters. Not so much the term I'd use, but that's beside the point. Many of you would so we're going to go with it. And while this might be true for you, I think we could all agree that there's a type of rollercoaster we'd call far from fun.

Expect Your Emotions to Be All Over the Place at Any Given Time

That's right. I'm talking about an emotional rollercoaster. As if our bodies going through a lot wasn't enough, our emotions are, too. Infertility essentially provokes an emotional rollercoaster. It may not look the same for every person, and it's definitely not going to look the same from day to day or even from minute to minute for one person alone. But everyone going through infertility will have some sort of emotional rollercoaster going on.

Take for example your hormones. Whether you're going through infertility or not, most women know that during certain parts in their cycle they are more emotional. They might be quicker to cry or get angry. They might be a bit touchier than normal so if one wrong thing was said (or even if the woman just took it wrong), they might fly off the handle. This is because our hormones fluctuate every day. These hormones can set our mood, control our mind, and even change our sanity. Factor in an infertility diagnosis and you've got emotions even more "out of whack".

Certain medications you may be taking, especially the hormonal kinds, will also cause some emotional ups and downs. Clomid, for example, is known to make women irritable. Some women even go as far as to say they are basically a witch while they're taking the pills. If you're getting shots that contain hormones, they can all do the same sort of thing. Anytime you mess with hormones, you will mess with emotions. Plus, the psychological part of why you're having to do this in the first place just really hits home and can make you depressed.

How long you've been walking this infertility journey will also determine some of your emotions. If you're just starting out, you might be in denial or possibly even still hopeful that your positive pregnancy test is just around the corner. Those that have been going on a couple of years or so might be in the "thick of it" for lack of a better phrase. At this stage you might be angrier, desperate, or even downright bitter. Those who have gone through infertility for years and years might have finally come to accept it and be numb to it. They might just be going through the motions. And, of course, any of these could be true for any stage of infertility, and will vary from person to person, as well as day to day. It all just depends on the person and their unique situation.

Speaking of what you're going through, how about life events? We can all think of at least a time or two when a certain event took place (or maybe even one we just heard about) that made us react emotionally. How about when you got engaged? I'm sure you felt happy and hopeful. How about when someone dies? You're torn in pieces and are filled with unbearable sadness. This same concept happens with infertility, but worse. For example, you find out what the issue is and you have a game plan in place. You'll definitely be hopeful it works! Maybe somewhere in your journey you did get a positive pregnancy test. Obviously, you're shocked, thrilled, and beyond yourself. On the flipside, your period just came. BOO! You might be depressed. You just heard that your best friend is pregnant with her first, second, third, or even fourth child. Heartbroken! (Although deep down there will be a tad of happiness. It's just not revealing itself at the moment.)

Some other factors that could affect your emotions are diet, sleep patterns, support system, etc. As women, we just need to accept the fact something as trivial as finding a dish in the sink when it should be in the dishwasher could make us go crazy.

One thing about emotional rollercoasters is that you could be completely fine one moment, but then something totally sets you off. Some hill, turn, or even upside-down thing just throws you for a loop. Although this isn't a complete list, here are some examples of things you may be feeling (and not all of them are negative):

- **Judgement.** You might judge the way people relate to their kids, judge how many kids they have, or even judge couples for getting pregnant fast. On the flip side, you might feel judgement from others regarding not having kids yet.

- **Jealousy.** This happened a lot for me. I wanted a baby so it only stands to reason I would get jealous when those around me got pregnant. I wanted what I didn't have.

- **Loneliness.** There may be days you feel no one understands you or is there to support you. Perhaps you're the only one in your social circle that is going through this so you just feel alone.

- **Hatred.** You hate what you're going through. You hate what you have to do just to get what you want. You hate other women for getting pregnant so fast. You may even hate God for making you go through infertility.

· **Anger.** This could be directed towards yourself, your spouse, the people around you, or even God.

· **Sadness.** I was always sad when I was going through infertility. Sad nothing worked and my period came. Sad I wasn't a mom yet. I was especially sad with the miscarriage, which was obviously expected.

· **Frustration.** This is how I felt every time someone I knew got pregnant, especially if they told me they weren't even trying, and especially if it was a teen who obviously wasn't ready for a baby yet.

· **Scared.** Maybe you just don't know what's going to happen next. Or perhaps you're going to start shots or a certain medication and are afraid of the side effects or the actual act of injecting yourself. I was scared to try and conceive again after the miscarriage because I definitely didn't want to go through that again.

· **Hope.** Every month there is a new hope, right? Maybe this will be the cycle you are finally successful! Maybe you'll have hope when there's a definitive diagnosis and a clear solution.

· **Happiness.** Ovulation time is always a happy time for various reasons. You might even be happy that something is working or going your way for a change.

· **Emptiness.** With no baby in your arms like those around you, you might feel empty. Or maybe you're just empty on the inside because you just have nothing left to give.

· **Defeated.** This is like emptiness where you have nothing left to give. You feel like you can't go on any longer. Maybe nothing is working and there's no clear direction to take. Maybe you just have lost all hope of ever conceiving.

· **Brokenness.** When our bodies don't work like they should, we feel broken. Our bodies were made to procreate, and because we can't, we must be broken. We need to be fixed. I know I've felt this way many times.

· **Lost.** This is typically a feeling we might get if we don't know which way to go. We might be at a crossroads of sorts.

· **Abandoned.** In the deepest parts of our journey, especially if we feel alone and don't think anyone gets what we're going through, we might feel like everyone's left us alone. When all our friends are getting pregnant, we feel left out in the dust. Worse yet, we may feel God doesn't care and has left us to fend for ourselves.

· **Resentment.** Infertility is unfair, and those going through it wholeheartedly agree. It's completely possible to resent others for not having to experience what you do.

· **Unstable.** You might be questioning everything that's going on. One moment you might be on board with something, but feel completely opposite sometime later. You're just unsure overall.

· **Cheated.** Women should be able to have babies, right? When we want them, but can't have them, we feel cheated out of the experience. Not just the pregnancy and birth, but a whole lifetime of memories.

· **Desperate.** Those going through infertility are usually willing to do whatever they have to do in order to get pregnant.

· **Guilty.** We feel like the ones to blame because we aren't getting pregnant. This is particularly true for female factor infertility where the fault truly does lie on us.

· **Excited.** You've ovulated and are experiencing some early pregnancy symptoms! That's exciting. Maybe it's even getting close to test time and you can't wait to pee on a stick. You might also be excited the day your period is supposed to show up, but it doesn't.

· **Content.** This might sound like a weird emotion to have in the midst of infertility, but it is completely possible. Some women strive to be completely content with God alone. There's nothing wrong with that, and I have to admit that is what I have been trying to live towards as well. However, I also know this isn't for everyone. But for those it is for, they are content to go through whatever it is God wants them to go through, knowing full well all that matters in the long run is their faith in Him.

· **Isolated.** A common thing to do during infertility is to not want to partake in various celebrations like baptisms or dedications, baby showers, or even Mother's Day. If we skip out on these things, which is understandable and okay to do, we might feel isolated. After all, we're shutting ourselves away from what's going on around us.

The list could go on and on and on. It's like the song that never ends, right? But this is true! There are so many emotions that go with the territory of infertility. There will be some ups and a lot of downs. You could feel all of these all at once or none of these at all. Perhaps there's a word not listed here that you would use to best describe how you feel. It's even possible you could feel some of these one moment and totally do a personality change the next moment. The point I want to make is that you'll go through an emotional rollercoaster. It doesn't matter what emotions they are for you. You just need to know every woman with infertility will have one to call their own. None of the emotions you experience are wrong or bad. All are understandable. All are normal.

The Five Stages of Grieving

Generally speaking, though, there tends to be a typical shift in our emotions. Most, if not all, of you have heard of the five stages of grieving. You know, the ones that Elisabeth Kubler Ross came up with in 1969 in her book, On Death and Dying. The five stages are denial, anger, bargaining, depression, and acceptance. This is basically the process humans go through when dealing with loss. There might be some bouncing back and forth between some of the stages as well, but overall, this is the general progression one will face.

All of these stages are true for infertility as well. After all, we have our own loss (that of not having a baby and missing out on a lifetime of memories with that child). Let me share with you how these five stages might apply to you as according to a page on RESOLVE's website. Please do check it out for more in-depth information.

· **Denial.** This could show itself in various ways. One might be to simply let people think you're fine when they ask about how you're doing.

Another example of denial is thinking your doctor or lab results are wrong. And yet a third way denial reveals itself is by simply continuing on your journey without any thought to what you've gone through the last cycle. I'm not saying dwell on your circumstances either, but we should allow ourselves a little bit of grieving. One thing I want to add to denial is that I think most of us do this without even realizing it. I can think of numerous times where people have asked how I was doing and I just say, "Good," or "Okay". I didn't do it out of denial so much (or maybe I'm denying my denial) as much as doing it out of the fact I don't feel like going into too much detail.

- **Anger.** "Why me?!?!" Sound familiar? Now that we aren't denying the issue any longer, we act out. It's not fair, right? In this phase, women can get angry at anyone. Usually it'll be women who are pregnant or who have children. But it's very possible to be mad at our partner, our doctors, or even the cashier at the local grocery store.

- **Bargaining.** In this phase, women going through infertility try to change themselves. They try to follow all the rules because they somehow think that is going to get them pregnant. It might be a diet they follow. Or perhaps they'll change their lifestyle. They implement whatever magic tricks they hear and think of because they believe it'll work. Take the comment, "You just need to relax," for example. Most of us know that relaxing isn't going to help one bit. But in this stage of grieving, you're going to relax as best you can because that just might be the trick.

- **Depression.** And now it's time to be sad. Things we used to find pleasurable won't be. We don't want to be around others, especially when it comes to baby showers and the like. We give up hope of anything working right. We want to give up trying. We do a lot of crying.

- **Acceptance.** Finally, we learn to accept that what is, is. It is this stage where most women will learn to be okay with their situation, knowing some day and in some way, everything will work out the way it was supposed to. This also happens to be the time where women are more open to the possibility of becoming a mom in a less traditional way such as through adoption. Some even decide to remain childless.

As a final word, I want to reiterate with you that there is no one size fits all when it comes to our emotions. We're not all identical, and are for sure not robots. It's common, understandable, okay, and even normal to have a bunch of different feels at any given point in time. Knowing that's a 100% true fact, please don't let anyone look down on you because you might be feeling differently than them or you're experiencing something they just don't understand. You have every right to feel what you feel when you feel it. Be sane or be a mess. Be sad or be happy. Be frustrated, happy, hateful, bitter, and content all at once. Be you! It's all okay. It's NORMAL! It comes with infertility's territory.

There's just one side note I want to make, and that is if you feel your emotions are getting the best of you and you might need professional help, please do not be afraid to research a place to seek counseling. I know help is out there should you need it.

Okay. How about we now move on from something less rocky and to something steamier? In the next chapter, you'll find one more thing you can expect for yourself as you go through infertility.

6

Let's Talk About Sex, Baby!

There's no denying that sex is an extremely important part of trying to get pregnant. After all, if you don't have sex, there are absolutely no chances of conceiving. Unless, of course, you were the virgin Mary. But this is a good thing because sex is fun, enjoyable, and proves to be a great bonding exercise. I mean, who doesn't like sex?

Enter in an infertility diagnosis.

Expect Your Sex Life to Change

The very definition of sex tends to change first. Instead of being seen as a recreational activity, it's now seen as an act that will hopefully allow us to procreate. One downside to infertility that goes along with this shift in thought is that your once spontaneous sex life will become, well, less spontaneous. Why? Because your sex life will not be whenever and wherever the mood strikes. It will now be timed in coordination with ovulation. I'm not saying you'll never have sex outside of that perimeter, but your fertile window will be go time for sure. I'm even willing to bet that if your partner happened to be away, and you just so happen to find out you're at your optimal fertile time, you'd probably do whatever you could to hightail his butt home.

Another way your sex life changes is that it becomes more boring. That may be a bit of a harsh word to use here, but, beyond sex being timed, it's also usually done in the same position over and over and over again. It gets old really fast.

Why do we do this to ourselves? Although there is no scientific proof, many people believe that certain sex positions are optimal to conceiving. The Bump, a handy resource dedicated to first time parents and parents to be, shared the down low on what those positions are and what they might do for you. Chances are, you're probably doing at least one of these because you've also heard the myths.

· **Missionary Style.** Many people believe this is ultimately the best way to conceive because not only can there be some decent penetration (the penis gets closer to the cervix), but you have gravity on your side. By laying down, the sperm don't have to try to swim upwards to get to the egg.

· **Hands-and-Knees (AKA Doggy Style).** This is the next preferred method in trying to conceive. This is by far the best way to get the deepest penetration imaginable. Those with a tipped uterus tend to benefit from this position better than missionary style because of the penetration aspect.

· **Woman on Top.** The only reason this one made the list is because this position is what brings some women the most pleasure, which in turn can be very effective in getting pregnant. The more pleasure you're receiving, the more cervical mucus your body tends to create. However, many believe that you'd be working against gravity here.

· **After-Sex Position.** What? That's not a sex position! Oh, yes, it is! When sex is done and over with, many people hold to the fact that women should prop their hips up on a small pillow for at least 20 minutes to help give the sperm just deposited into the vagina some help getting into and up the uterus. I actually found myself doing this quite often. I don't recall if any of those times resulted in me getting pregnant, though. I do remember it being such a chore as it was boring and rendered me useless.

Now, keep in mind, these are all myths. The reasoning behind each of these do sound legit, but there is not hardcore proof. After all, sex is sex. No matter what position you try, if you're ovulating and you've had intercourse, you have a fair shot of getting pregnant.

Variety Is the Spice of Life

If you're finding yourself in a rut with your partner and the sex life you two are sharing, there are many ways to spice things up. But before I dish out some of those ideas, I want to emphasize that some negativity surrounding sex and infertility is far deeper than just being boring and unspontaneous. With infertility comes a lot of hurt and other tough feelings, and at times it could even be at your partner for one reason or another. This will equate to no sex or downright bad sex. Well, maybe not bad sex. I'm not sure if there is such a thing when it comes to two willing partners. Maybe I should say mutually-fulfilling sex, as in if there are deeper issues going on, it won't be mutually fulfilling. If that is the case for you, what will help in this area is open honesty and excellent communication about anything and everything. For those who might not be able to see an improvement on your own, please don't hesitate to seek help in some way.

Okay. So here is a list of some unique ways to spice up your sex life:

· **Change positions!** For the third time, there is no scientific proof that you have to have missionary style sex all the time just to get pregnant. So, mix things up a bit! If you find something far more pleasurable, do it! If you want to try something completely new, do it! Just don't hurt yourself. Bottom line, aim for variety in your positions.

· **Foreplay!** Not only is foreplay fun, but it builds up excitement in both partners. Getting excited gets the juices flowing so take time touching, kissing, tickling, sucking, rubbing, and what have you, all areas of your partner's body.

· **Change location!** I know that sex on the bed is the most comfortable way to have sex. At least for me. But that doesn't mean that has to be the only place you have sex! Especially during the day when the bed may not be accessible, don't wait. Do it where you are! Try a new spot you haven't christened yet. Try the car! If you're really daring, do it in public somehow! Although, do be sure you aren't caught because that is illegal.

· **Use toys!** This isn't something that I would feel comfortable using, but many of you out there do have them and thoroughly enjoy them. That's great! If it's something that gives you and your partner a lot of satisfaction, go for it! Make sure they are clean when used of course.

· **Try food!** Sometimes this can be very messy, but it's a lot of fun. Cool whip will limit the messiness, but try a variety of things such as peanut butter, chocolate syrup, or even honey. Go for a combination! Whatever floats your boat here. The object is to put it on the person and clean them off by using your tongue! Super arousing.

· **Massage each other's naked bodies!** And I don't mean a quick rub to get it over with. When my husband and I do this, we time each other. We each have to massage the other for 15 minutes. Not only does this feel good and relaxing, but it builds anticipation as you near the more intimate parts. I can guarantee you that each and every time you do this you will end up having sex – amazing sex!

· **Set the mood!** I know this isn't always feasible because you just want a quickie. That's all fine and dandy. But for those times when sex might be a little more planned out, at least make the most of it. You can set the mood with music, lighting, what you're wearing, etc.

· **Fulfill a fantasy!** This one can be really fun! Get whatever props you want and act out a fantasy you or your partner dream about! Maybe even videotape the experience! Either way, as long as you're both comfortable with it, have fun living it up.

· **Play a game!** No, I'm not talking about a board game, although you might be able to find some adult/naughty-ish board games out there. I have some game ideas you can use that require items you probably already have at home, are super fun, and will get you in the mood and ready for a fun time.

   o **Naughty Cards.** All you need for this game is a deck of cards. You will assign a certain activity to each suit. For example, hearts can be kissing, diamonds can be massaging, clubs can be manual stimulation, and spades oral stimulation. And then the number will correspond to the number of seconds you have to do said activity. Go back and forth, each partner taking their turn by picking a card and performing as they need to. So, for example, if you pick a seven of hearts, you would kiss your partner for seven seconds. Make sense? It's a lot of fun!

   o **X Marks the Spot.** You just need your bodies for this one. All you have to do is think of a special spot, and then your partner's job is to kiss you in various places until they find the spot you were thinking of. Then switch turns. Now, whether you choose to be honest here or not is your choice. For a lot of people, the kissing feels so good they just keep their partner guessing.

o **Dirty Drawings.** Your inner artist will thank you for this one. It's super simple doing this one. Just grab a pencil and paper and draw your partner naked. In turn, let them draw you naked. It's neat seeing what you both come up with. Studying each other's bodies while drawing will make your mind (and heart) race.

o **Kinky Dice.** You'll need to make a chart for this one, as well as get out two dice. On the top, label your columns one through six. Do the same for your rows. Then fill each inner square with a sexual activity. There can be some free spaces if you wish. Basically, you roll one dice. That's your row. Roll the second dice. That's your column. Or vice versa. However, you want to do it is fine. Before you start, make sure you have an agreeable amount of time you want to do each activity. Whatever spot you land on will equal what you have to do for your partner. Then switch turns!

o **Pick a Card.** This is like Kinky Dice. On slips of paper, write pleasurable sexual activities. Either have a set time or make a second set of slips of paper with different times. Each partner takes a turn picking a paper and revealing what they have to do with their lover for a set amount of time.

o **Sextagories.** This game requires some thinking and creativity, but will definitely put your mind in the right direction for sex. Sextagories is like Scattergories in that you have a list of ten items. Then you go down that list thinking of a word that fits starting with a letter that has been chosen. You can pick a random letter, or if you have Scattergories, you can use the dice that comes with that. Here's the list that I use:

§ A Body Part

§ A Sexual Position

§ A Place You Would Have Sex

§ A Place You Like to Kiss

§ Another Word for Sex

§ A Place You Like to Rub

§ Something That Happens During Sex

§ A Sex Act

§ A Dirty Word

§ Another Word for Penis/Vagina

Once you get the letter chosen, each answer on this list would need to start with that letter. For example, if the letter was "M", you could answer: for one, muscle; two, missionary; three, mom's house; and so on and so on.

There are so many other games, or even ways for that matter, that you could implement when it comes to sex. Get creative, have fun, explore, get down and dirty. Do whatever you need to do to light the fire in your sex life!

Work It

Here's something to consider. An article on <u>Verywell</u> regarding spicing up your sex life stated that research has shown that the more aroused a person is, the better chances they have of getting pregnant. For men, they tend to produce more sperm. And for women, they tend to produce more cervical fluids. And we all know that if a woman has more cervical fluids, there is a better chance for the sperm released in her to get the help they need to go where they need to go. Therefore, if you are one to try everything in the book to increase your chances of pregnancy, you'll probably work your tail off to make sex as exciting as possible.

Now I know there are some of you out there that have not and will not see a difference in your sex life. That's the "beauty" of infertility; not every case of it is the same. So, for those that saw/see no difference, I'm hoping you could still learn something. Maybe even try something different just because!

There are also a few of you that saw your sex life get better because of infertility. After all, sex is great and you're having tons of it, right? And that's awesome! I'm glad your sex life has improved.

However, the majority of us saw a downturn, which is why this chapter is so necessary. A stale sex life, on top of all the negative feelings that come with the ugliness that infertility is, will take a lot of work to get things back to the way things were. But the good thing is, the women who have all gone through this before know that it's completely possible!

There's another great positive to working on our sex lives beyond more arousal, trying something new, having fun, etc. And that is we will really get to know our partner on the deepest level possible. We'll get a greater sense of what they like, and what they don't like so much. We'll get a feel for what makes them tick. And the truth is vice versa also! It's a great feeling when your partner is so in tune with you, and just connects with you on every level.

With all of this said, I know there are many of you who may be too tired, uncomfortable, depressed, or just in place of an "I don't care" attitude to even want to make a difference in your sex life. At this point you may feel there's no use trying, or perhaps you're not even bothered by the type of sex life you have. And that's okay! I completely understand what you're going through. All you've got to do is throw out the window everything I just said. My feelings won't be hurt one bit. I know that you really don't need one more thing to work on, on top of everything infertility related.

There's no one size fits all when it comes to infertility and what you'll feel or experience. Every journey is going to be different, and so some things that appeal to you may or may not appeal to someone else, and vice versa. Some things that you might want to try working on may or may not be an area another woman needs to address. My goal in this chapter, and really throughout the entire book, is to simply inspire you in some way on something. Whether it's to help you let go, have more fun, show you something new, or whatever, I hope you come away feeling more in control of your situation than before you started reading this book.

Part Three

***

What to Expect from Everyone Else

7

The Male Factor

We've covered some things that you can expect for yourself on this infertility journey. Now let's transition to what you can expect from the people around you. Why not start with the person closest to you on this journey: your partner? After all, your man plays a pretty important role in the whole baby-making process. And, whether you realize it or not, your man also is going through a lot while the two of you are waiting for that special bundle of joy to arrive.

Expect Your Man to Be Affected

Yes, it's true that your man will be going through a tough time just like you are. He, too, feels left out, has to go through testing, deal with inferior results, and, most importantly, live without what he deeply desires: a baby.

There are three main ways the men in the relationship are affected. Let's examine them now.

- **Physically.** When people think of infertility or see infertile couples, it's extremely common to think that it's the female's problem. After all, we are the ones not getting larger every month due to a baby inside us just gearing up to make its way into the world. Because we aren't popping out kids, many automatically assume it's our fault. Or we are the ones that have an issue. And guess what, friends? Nothing could be farther from the truth!

    Like I had previously mentioned in an earlier chapter, of couples that are struggling with infertility, 30% are due to the man in the equation. This is the same percentage that was assigned to females being the sole issue. What the statistics mean is that just as many men are the problem as women.

    What causes male infertility? RESOLVE listed a variety of things on their website, such as "structural abnormalities, sperm production disorders, ejaculatory disorders, and immunologic disorders". So basically, anything from their "package" to "swimmers" to "bodily juices" to immune system can all be the culprit.

This kind of sounds familiar. I mean, women can have all of those issues as well that leads to female infertility. We can have issues with our reproductive system structure and function, and we definitely are not immune to immune system disorders. So, it appears to me that we are all kind of in the same boat physically-wise.

· **Emotionally.** No, they may not shed as many tears as us women do. But that doesn't mean they're not struggling. Remember all the emotions you may experience from day to day or even minute to minute? Your man is feeling them, too. It's just that oftentimes the man's feelings get overlooked due to the infertility-is-a-female's-problem stigma.

Feelings of guilt, anger, and low self-esteem tend to weigh heavily on a man dealing with infertility. Why? Because just like women get wrapped up in feeling less than a woman because she can't reproduce, so a man feels less of a man because he can't get a woman pregnant. So much of a man's existence is defined in being fertile. When, of course, there's an issue, their masculinity has been assaulted.

Men also struggle with feeling helpless. Whether it be that the cause lies on them or they just see the tough time their partner is going through, there's one common theme. They can't do a thing to fix the situation. Try as they might, so often they fail. That, again, tends to go against everything they were taught constitutes as a real man.

Being overwhelmed is another big feeling men experience. The decisions to make, tests to take, financial costs, and add on top of that the plethora of emotions their partners have, as well as the ones they themselves are feeling, is a recipe for overflow. It can be way too much for one person to handle.

These "manly" emotions only scratch the surface. I'm willing to bet that whatever you're feeling, your man probably is, too.

· **Relationally.** The best relationship your man has is probably with you. However, when going through infertility, they can feel the strain as much as you do. Especially when it comes to coping methods, understanding one another, and trying to figure out which direction to take, there's bound to be butting of heads. Regarding sex, they, too, are aware it has changed. Some men wish it would go back to the way it was and other men might be plain old tired from having too much sex because you're peak fertile window has arrived.

Just like with women, men will even struggle in their relationship with God. They can't possibly understand why God wouldn't let him be able to procreate. The pressures and demands of an infertility struggle may make faith in God very hard.

And what about everyone else? Men are just as likely to become jealous with their peers if they are able to have kids while he can't. So, they, too, might stay away from them. They are just as likely to be burdened on Father's Day as women are on Mother's Day because it's just another reminder that they aren't a father yet. So, they, too, may choose to stay away from the celebrations. Also, men tend to not give too much detail in their conversations so they may feel a lack of help from others or unsupported all together.

In general, all of your man's relationships will be affected. For those that do know what you and your man are going through, those relationships might become awkward, and your husband may feel embarrassed or ashamed when around them. And for those that have no clue what the two of you are going through, those relationships might be more guarded so they never do find out.

Now, having just said that, these situations and examples may not always be the case. And there will undoubtedly be a person or two (hopefully more) that are super close to you and your man that will actually help you get through this tough time. But don't be surprised if you begin to realize some of what I just shared with you is taking/has taken place.

I hope that you can see that, just like you, your man has a lot to deal with. He's got emotions to process and a lot of unknowns. It's hard for him to not give you a baby, and/or to see you so hurt. So, it's not that you're going through anything different or that either one of you don't feel what the other one feels. The only difference between you and your partner is how you go about handling everything.

Expect Your Man to Cope Differently

Georgia Reproductive Specialists have a website, www.ivf.com, that is dedicated to not only the services they provide, but also to providing information on infertility and the things that come with it. They shared a good point on their article, "The Emotional Effects of Infertility on the Couple Relationship," that I think bears repeating. It was that women tend to be seen as the emotional caretakers or providers of the relationship. Whereas men tend to be seen as the protectors and financial providers of the relationship.

Taking that into consideration, as well as the basic fact men were created different from women, we can begin to see the truth behind how each partner will cope with infertility. Where women feel free to show their emotions in one way or another, men tend to do one or more of the following four things:

· **Become fixers.** Men are trained to solve problems. Infertility is a problem. Your man may be doing things to help "fix" the issue, whether it be trying to make you feel better or going above and beyond what's required of him because he feels he'll do anything and everything to help you get pregnant. Those who are fixers will also take charge with decisions because, in their mind, by doing so, they are going to see the fruit of those decisions equal a baby.

· **Become bottle-uppers.** Most men put on a brave face no matter what is going on in their life. And most men wouldn't dare let others see them cry or in emotional pain. Instead, they'll just bear the weight of your emotions as well as their own, pretending everything is okay.

· **Become minimalizers.** This one may seem harsh, but it's really not. Some men tend to belittle the situation because they just can't take the overwhelming feelings you both have. So minimalizers tend to move on from a depressing moment, holding to the hope that whatever you do next will work. It's not that they didn't care. It's just that they don't want to believe the issue you're both facing is insurmountable because that would really damage his pride.

· **Become sidetrackers.** Most, if not all men, when faced with something they just don't know how to handle, will throw their entire attention elsewhere, particularly where they do see success. These types of men will work more or tinker around more often. Basically, anything that can keep them busy, they will find and do. This allows them to be sidetracked and not have to think about their present dire situation.

Keep in mind that not all men will be like this. Some men are able to express how they're feeling and what they're going through with no problem. Some men have no problems crying and talking about their hardships. And there are even a very, very few who perhaps aren't as bothered by infertility like you are so they act nonchalant because they really are nonchalant.

But the opposite is true, too! Some women exhibit these traits themselves. There are plenty of women out there that hide their thoughts and emotions and/or do whatever they can to stay busy and not address the issue at hand. And rare, but true, there are instances where the man is more affected by everything than the woman. The only reason this information was posted here was because generally women can and do show emotions while men generally do not.

And that's okay! Please know that no way of coping is a wrong way, as long as you're not harming yourself or someone else. Whichever way you need to process the things you're going through, do it. Just remember that your way may not be your partner's way and vice versa. As a couple, you'll need to realize that so that you can be there for one another.

Just the Two of Us

RESOLVE made a good point when they said that infertility is a couples' problem. It should never be seen as a man's issue or woman's issue. It is a couples' issue, and because of that, the couple needs to work as a team through it. Together.

If you are finding that things have been off between you and your partner due to miscommunication or a lack of understanding one another and where you're both coming from when dealing with how infertility is being handled, Georgia Reproductive Specialists, in the same article listed above, has a few good tips to implement that will hopefully help you reconnect.

· Communicate openly with one another.

· Realize there's no right or wrong way to feel.

· Get in touch with how you feel so you can figure out what you need. Then clearly and specifically tell your partner how they can help.

· Ask your partner what they need instead of assuming you already know.

· Recognize the psychological and emotional differences between the two of you.

· Teach one another the skills you've learned from your own experiences.

· Share your burdens and joys. Share your perceptions and experiences with infertility. It will help bring you closer with a deeper respect for each other.

Here's one last tip. I like what best-selling author, Gary Thomas, said in his book, Sacred Marriage. He pointed out that couples need to fully respect in order to understand. Once they understand they can fully love. Isn't that a beautifully true statement? This, of course, goes with all aspects of your relationship, but I can see it really coming in handy when dealing with infertility. We should all fully respect our partners and what they, too, are going through and/or how they are doing it. This way we'll understand, and in turn, fully love them.

As a final thought, it may not always be the case, but your partner should be your strongest support, as should you be his. Infertility is no fun for anyone involved. And it has and will ruin marriages. I've seen it happen many times before. Therefore, I encourage you to cling to your partner. Seek to be open and honest while also being respectful and understanding so that your relationship can flourish. This way neither of you will be left feeling pushed to the side or overburdened.

After all, your partner is all you have who has the best clue as to what you're dealing with.

8

People Say the Darndest Things

Do you remember the TV show called <u>Kids Say the Darndest Things?</u> Or have you at least heard the phrase? I know it gets used often. Anyway, this show was hosted by <u>Bill Cosby</u> in the late 90s, and what made it a hit for a short time was the fact kids really come up with some funny things to say. Each show, <u>Bill Cosby</u> would ask kids certain questions, and you could be sure there would be at least one answer that would crack you up. Obviously, it's because they simply don't understand.

Well, this concept holds true for adults as well. When talking about something we don't really know the full scope of, we tend to say some pretty interesting things, some of which can be funny. But when it comes to infertility, it's far from it; it's actually downright offensive or foolish.

In life, there are just some things you can't control. For example, the weather, our government, death, illness, and so many other things, are going to do what it wants when it wants to, whether we like it or not. The same is true for those suffering from infertility. We can't control our bloodwork and/or test results. We can't prevent miscarriages from happening. We can't even control when we get pregnant in the first place. If we could, we certainly wouldn't be infertile, now would we?

So why do people say things that make it seem that they think we can control those things? What is it about infertility that makes people say things that are utterly stupid?

Expect Unwanted Questions and Advice

People talk. A lot! And many people will do it without anyone even listening! It's my opinion that people just like to hear themselves and find it very difficult to be quiet. Even when it comes to speaking on things referring to a disease, like infertility, they just can't help themselves.

As some examples, have you ever heard any (or all) of these statements?

· **"So, when are you going to have a baby?"** This one gets asked all the time, especially if you've been married for quite a while. The two-year mark really raises peoples' curiosity if there's no baby on your hip yet. Since when did it even become our right to know when another couple will try for a baby? Other couples' fertility is not our business! Every time I hear it spew out of someone's mouth I cringe, and it's become my personal goal to not even ask this question because it can bring on hurtful feelings. You just never know if that person has been trying for years, or if they just had a failed IVF attempt, or if they have been told recently their best bet would be to adopt. Let's do other women a favor and just not worry about when they will have a baby! It's just not our place!

· **"You just need to relax!"** Really? That's all I need to do? Like being relaxed is going to instantly get me pregnant and help me pop out a kid in nine months? UGH! No, none of this is true. Don't you just want to slap someone for saying that, though? I know I did. Those who say this make it seem like it is completely our fault when it's not. And no amount of relaxing techniques or expensive vacations we may go on will magically get us pregnant. Now, it is true that some women have gotten pregnant on a vacation, and it could very well have been because they were more relaxed, but this is rare. Relaxing does not equal babies.

· **"You can always adopt!"** Hmm. Last time I checked, I don't think it's entirely possible for just any average joe to adopt a baby. Not only is there a mountain high stack of papers that need to be filled out, but there are many home studies you need to pass, and other legalities to work out. And, perhaps the biggest deterrent to adopting, is the cost factor! An article on Adoption.com, an excellent resource for anything adoption related, did a great job laying out the costs of adoption. There aren't two cases that will be the same, but depending the route you take, you can have costs up to and greater than $40,000! That's a lot of money, folks! Add on top of that the fact that as many as a third of adoptive parents experienced a false start (coming close to the adoption being final, but the whole situation goes bad in the end), and that is so frustrating and heartbreaking. Also, I do have to say that not all couples have it in their heart to adopt anyway, and there's nothing wrong with that. So, no, you can't always just adopt.

· **"God has a plan."** This is very true. God does have a plan, and I know that He will see to it that everything goes according to it. However, when people say this, they are essentially saying that what we're going through isn't a big deal. They are belittling our struggles, emotions, thoughts, plans, expectations, desires, etc. I've said this before, infertility is really tough. Those suffering from it aren't saying God doesn't have a plan. There are just saying that His plan hurts for the moment.

· **"God won't give you more than you can handle."** I think this statement is the most false and abused biblical statement that you will ever come across. Nowhere in the Bible does this phrase even exist. This is what the Bible really says: "The temptations in your life are no different from what others experience. And God is faithful. He will not allow the temptation to be more than you can stand. When you are tempted, he will show you a way out so that you can endure" (1 Corinthians 10:13).

First of all, did this verse indicate anything about suffering at all? No, it refers to temptations. Second of all, when some says this, they are essentially saying that God knows how much you can take until you'll break, and then when you get to that point, your suffering will stop. I'm not denying that God doesn't know how much we can take or can't take, but a website titled What Christians Want to Know did an article on this verse, stating, "Many times this simply encourages the person undergoing the difficulty to look inward and think that he or she is strong enough to handle whatever comes up because God has promised a limit to their struggles. It is believed that we have all we need already inside us."

This article went on to say, "However; this can, and often does, have the effect of turning the focus upon oneself instead of on God, where it should be. The person begins to rely on himself instead of looking to God for strength. This can lead to self-dependence instead of God-dependence. We can unwittingly stop relying on God for our strength because we have begun to rely on our self for it instead."

When someone says this to you, again, they are using incorrect theology and you shouldn't listen. Instead, use this verse to remind you that our strength comes from God, and however your infertility situation plays out, He's in it and with you.

· **"At least you're getting some good practice!"** Practice here is referring to sex, and there tends to be a lot of that going on when you're trying to have a kid. However, this statement again denies the bigger issue. Why, yes, we get a lot of practice, but so what? That's not really what we want in the first place! I actually got this phrase a couple of times right after I miscarried our first baby. Each time the person expressed their condolences (and then should have stopped there), but then went on to utter, "At least you're getting a lot of practice." And they have this huge smile on their face to boot! Cue annoyed eye roll.

· **"At least you've got one already."** This statement is only directed at those going through secondary infertility. People tend to believe that secondary infertility sufferers should still be happy because they at least have one child. This also tends to be why this infertility sub-group is unfortunately often pushed to the side. They're seen as inferior to primary infertility sufferers because those people have nothing. However, regardless of infertility type, it's tough. Those dealing with secondary infertility, I know you're still struggling just as much as the others so I have a suggestion. If you find yourself the recipient of this atrocious comment, ask them a question in return. Say, "Would you cut off one of your legs?" Obviously that person will say, "No." Then politely respond with, "Why? You've already got one. Isn't that enough?" After that you might want to just walk away so you don't do anything incriminating.

· **"There are worse things that could happen."** Death and dying may be the only things worse than wanting a baby and not being able to have one. We don't know what exactly each couple is going through when they are suffering from infertility so infertility could very well be the worst thing to them. Saying something this idiotic is just cruel in my honest opinion.

· **"At least you can sleep in late,"** or **"At least you have the two of you,"** or **"At least you'll get to do a lot of traveling."** Each of these statements and all similar ones like it just minimalize the situation. I mean, you wouldn't tell someone who has lost a mom, "Hey, at least you don't have to buy a Mother's Day card anymore." Same thing with these examples. They shouldn't be said. They do nothing but belittle what the sufferer is going through.

There are probably many more comments you could add to this list, but you catch my drift here. People will say what they want when they want it, most being empty words. And it really all boils down to not being able to control their tongues. When something happens, it's in our nature to have to say something. In fact, James 3:2-10 clearly states, "Indeed, we all make many mistakes. For if we could control our tongues, we would be perfect and could also control ourselves in every other way. We can make a large horse go wherever we want by means of a small bit in its mouth. And a small rudder makes a huge ship turn wherever the pilot chooses to go, even though the winds are strong. In the same way, the tongue is a small thing that makes grand speeches. But a tiny spark can set a great forest on fire. And among all the parts of the body, the tongue is a flame of fire. It is a whole world of wickedness, corrupting your entire body. It can set your whole life on fire, for it is set on fire by hell itself. People can tame all kinds of animals, birds, reptiles, and fish, but no one can tame the tongue. It is restless and evil, full of deadly poison. Sometimes it praises our Lord and Father, and sometimes it curses those who have been made in the image of God. And so, blessing and cursing come pouring out of the same mouth. Surely, my brothers and sisters, this is not right!"

Does this make it right for people to say the things they do to us? No. But at least there's somewhat a reason why they do. Our best bet is to politely respond and then walk away, making a mental note not to cross paths with that person for a while again. Or if you're up to it, lovingly correct and educate them!

But also, I have to admit that we are all guilty of this at one point in our lives or another. There are things that I have said that I realized later was not the best thing. There are times I have kicked myself for talking without thinking. I'm sure you have been there, too. Everyone has. And, honestly, while some people may not care, I firmly believe that the majority of people that say these things are not trying to be harsh. I know I'm never trying to be harsh when I speak incorrectly. Most times there is good intentions. The only thing lacking is understanding.

9

They Just Don't Get It

Remember back in part two of this book where I went through some things you should expect for yourself? And remember I mentioned at the beginning of that section that infertility was like a club? Well, we're going to circle back to that analogy in this chapter.

What makes infertility a club is that, unless you have gone through it yourself, you'll never understand what it's like. Sure, you might have a general idea or you might be able to correctly express your sympathy, but you won't totally get it. What exactly won't you get? Besides all the tests, appointments, failures, etc., you wouldn't understand the core of what makes infertility what it is.

Infertility sufferers have this great need, and that is to have a baby. Because this must-have-children mentality that infertile couples have cannot and will not be matched, there will be discrepancies on how people view those couples, what they're going through, and the decisions they make.

And I'm not trying to say that people around you are evil and are purposely trying to be mean or insensitive (although some might be). What I am trying to say is that they simply don't understand, and therefore, their views will be different.

Expect Others to Not Fully Understand

Let's go through a variety of situations to see how your view may differ from that of a non-infertile person. Keep in mind, please, that everyone handles their journey differently. Some of these situations may not affect you the way they do others. Also, there may be some really awesome people out there that are more in tune with what us infertility sufferers are going through so they might not feel the way I'm about to share. These examples/situations are just a generality that provide proof that others just don't get it.

- **Skipping celebrations.** When I say celebrations, I am referring to all the ones related to babies or moms. So, it could be child dedications or baptisms, baby showers, Mother's Day get-togethers, etc. For those that are dealing with infertility, it's super common to want to skip out on them. It's hard having to go through something that just further reiterates your condition and what you don't have. I'm not saying you aren't happy for those having baby showers or those who are offering their kid to God. What I am saying is that you constantly wish it was you doing those things. Not just being some innocent bystander.

Do you know what others might think, though, if you choose to not participate? They might see you being rude or selfish. They're going to tell you they get it, but deep down they're going to wonder why you couldn't put your problem aside to celebrate them and their child for just one day.

When I was in the deepest part of my infertility journey, I just could not do baby showers. That was my breaking point. I could handle Mother's Day and baptisms or dedications, but baby showers? No, that was going too far. However, each time I chose to deny going, more than one person would make me feel like the lowliest of lows. Sure, they said, "Okay." They even told me they would miss me. But that all came after they tried manipulating me into going.

One thing I want you to remember is that if you are one of those that don't want to partake in the festivities that go on around having children, it's okay. Hopefully no one will make you feel bad for it, but if they do, it's because they don't understand what a gut-wrenching, heart-breaking, soul-crushing experience it would be for you.

· **Keeping certain plans.** This applies to those choosing to commit to scheduled activities, usually sex, instead of venturing off to something else. Maybe it's a weekend night and you're offered to go to a party or to hang out with special friends. Maybe there's even someone else who really needs you at the moment. However, you know for a fact you're ovulating and you and your partner just have this one night to try and make a baby so you decline. Now, whether you tell them why you're declining is up to you, but regardless of that piece of information, they may not understand.

For you, skipping out on this delicacy is necessary. Everything could be delayed another month if you were to not keep these plans. To them, they might think you're no fun, you're boring, you're a party pooper, or the like. Some might ask you, "What's gotten into you?" Others might say, "I wish you hadn't changed." No matter how hard it is to even say no to them, trust me, they'll get over it at some point.

· **Stopping treatments.** I know you might be highly puzzled by reading that. Let me explain. At some point, those going through infertility stop what they're going through. It could be because they got pregnant. It could be because they decided adoption was the way to go. Or it could be that they decided to stay a family of two. Either way, treatments cannot go on forever.

For those who still haven't gotten pregnant, and yet decide to stop treatments, most people are going to question how much you really wanted that baby. You'll get a handful of people urging you to keep trying; to never give up. That's great advice and all, but what they don't realize is how tough the decision to stop treatments was in the first place. They need support, not criticism.

There are countless other situations you will most undoubtedly find yourself in where your views/decisions will not line up with those around you. This is because people just don't get our obsession (and this obsession is not a bad thing)! They certainly try to, though. I believe people do care, and that their intentions are inherently good. But your priority will not be their priority, and therefore, their words/actions will not always come off as such.

And what do you get when people don't fully understand things the way you do? People who say and do the wrong things. Not because they want to, mind you, but that won't stop it from hurting.

Expect No One to Handle Your Suffering Correctly

In the last chapter, we already covered the fact that people will say the wrong things to those who are going through infertility. Some of it may be because they think they are helping you. Some of the things they say could be because they heard it before and thought they'd share their wealth of knowledge. Some of it could be because they're just curious. No matter what the reason may be, the underlying root is all due to not understanding the situation.

Do you remember the old phrase, "Sticks and stones may break my bones, but words will never hurt me?" The truth is, words can actually be pretty hurtful. But beside that point, I do agree that actions can also break us pretty badly. You would know because I'm sure at least one of these acts have been done to you:

- **Nothing.** What I mean here is that people won't say or do anything to you in regard to what you're going through. It's not like they'll stop talking to you or won't want to be around you, but they will pretend you don't have this big gaping hole in your heart because of what you're struggling with. They don't want to mention anything out of fear it could be the wrong thing to say. They don't show any kind of support because they're just not sure what to do or what would even make you feel better.

  I can sort of understand their logic. When something makes me uncomfortable, I tend to shy away from it as well. I don't want to be around something I don't get. But what this essentially shows the person going through a great pain is that you either don't care or that what they're going through isn't that big of a deal. Actions alone can really make a sufferer feel loved and valued or completely forgotten and left out.

- **Denial.** This is kind of like doing nothing, but with a slight twist. Have you ever had something happen to you, but the people around you simply choose to ignore it? Not all together, of course, because it's not like we're barbarians. These people might ask you how something went or they might listen to what you've said about something on your journey, but then either they show no sympathy whatsoever or they quickly pass it off and move on to something more uplifting.

  As an example, when I had my miscarriage, I was going to a very tiny church at the time. There were only three other women my age, two of which were married. One of them happened to get pregnant a few weeks after I did even though they were not trying and had wanted to wait a little longer. Well, I lost my baby. Yes, the church knew, and, yes, they all expressed their condolences. But after that one moment, it was all about this other woman who was still pregnant. People didn't talk with me as much. No one really knew how to go about mourning with me. And, no, it's not like I wanted everyone to dwell on it, but I did want to be acknowledged.

Whether it's a failed attempt with IUI/IVF, or a miscarriage, or an adoption placement gone wrong, or whatever it may be, if people act like this didn't happen to you, you definitely feel unimportant; like you and your situation doesn't matter. You'll feel alone because you're going to think you have no support. I know I felt that way.

· **Convene.** If you could go 180 degrees in the total opposite direction, this would be it. Instead of sticking to the notion it's best to barely poke your head into our struggles, these people call up the "troops" and "love" on you. On the surface this looks like a really great thing, doesn't it? After all, it's nice when people acknowledge our journey and the fact that we are having a tough time in certain areas and with certain things. However, sometimes it's either too much or it is simply not what we're looking for at all.

As an example, I have to go back to that church I was attending when I had my miscarriage. Like I said before, I felt like they denied anything ever happened to me. After a couple of months of really trying to come to grips with the fact I was no longer pregnant, but one other woman in the church was, a few members realized I was not okay. So, what did they decide to do? Throw a miscarriage party! Okay. It wasn't a party, but I really can't think of a better word.

Basically, what happened was they had me go to a meeting that consisted of the other women in the church who have had a miscarriage before. Then, as we sat in a circle in someone's living room, each woman rehashed their story. Now, I'm not trying to say their story wasn't important, but having them tell me what they went through didn't help me one tiny bit. I felt bad for them, sure. But that doesn't make me feel better about my situation. Especially since none of them had gone through infertility before so really had no clue what I was truly facing.

You might have a group of girls that you're really close with that might decide to get together with you and pamper you. If that's your sort of thing then that's pretty neat. For others, like myself, it can be emotionally draining. Trying to get a bunch of people together to pounce on someone else is just never a good idea no matter what it's for. At least that's my opinion.

There are probably many other examples we could go through, all of which indicate the same underlying theme of others not understanding infertility and how those with it cope with it. People just simply don't know how to "weep with those who weep" (Romans 12:15). The being happy part found just before this phrase in the Bible no one has an issue with. The weeping part is where people either scratch their heads or choose to look the other way.

Proper Infertility Etiquette

Unfortunately, we can't change how people act towards us. But we can change the way we act towards others. This is why I want to share some of the following ideas with you. You can find these helpful for any situation that involves someone going through a tough time, be it infertility, a sickness, a severe injustice, you get the point.

- **Practice Shiva.** Do you know what that is? Shiva is the Jewish custom for mourning. Those who have lost a person close to them will partake in Shiva. Would you like to know what's interesting about those who go to visit a person practicing Shiva? Look at how they act:

    o They enter the home quietly.

    o They don't say a single word unless the person practicing Shiva engages with them. And what they do say is severely limited, usually just to express condolences.

    o They are aware of the atmosphere so that they act in a way that is not going to offend the person who is mourning.

    o They provide food.

To me, this is such a beautiful way to express support for someone, and what is so cool about Shiva is that it can be used in many situations. It's all about being present and providing without making it about yourself. It's about being available, should the need arise, without offending. For other information on Shiva such as how to practice it or how to act with those who are going through it, check out the website, Shiva.com.

This practice reminds me of what my dad did for me when I had my miscarriage. He came to the house quietly. He didn't say a whole lot. He didn't bring a meal, but he did bring this beautiful flower basket. And he just sat with us. That example was so precious to me that I have incorporated that into what I do should I know someone that's gone through a miscarriage.

And remember, this doesn't have to be limited to miscarriages or other kinds of losses. You can easily do this for someone going through a divorce or who has been sick for a long time.

· **Be slow to speak.** This little phrase comes from James 1:19, which fully states, "Understand this, my dear brothers and sisters: You must all be quick to listen, slow to speak, and slow to get angry." Instead of jumping to conclusions or assuming things may be a certain way or a person feels a certain feeling, take time to just listen. The other person may not say anything at all, but even in their silence, they are speaking volumes. I think the world would be a much better place if we took the time to listen and not speak. Don't you think that's why God gave us two ears, but just one mouth? Listen! And really get to know the truth before speaking.

· **Remember.** When I first started going to the church I currently attend, I quickly found out how big of a deal they made Mother's Day and Father's Day. For Mother's Day, they would have all the moms stand up, get a huge shout and round of applause, as well as get prayed over. For Father's Day, it was the same thing, but just for dads instead of moms. I'm glad they understand that being a mom or dad is a big deal. However, there was little consideration for how those aspiring to be those things felt.

The leaders in the church got wind of how some women/men felt in regard to these two holidays and how the church went about celebrating them. And now? The scene is much different. There's still a round of applause, which I feel moms and dads deserve on occasion, and moms/dads are still asked to stand up. But the best part is that during the little tribute to moms/dads and during the prayer, there is now mention of those going through infertility (those wanting to be moms/dads). No one is singled out anymore, in my opinion, and the suffering are remembered. When this shift happened before I had my first child, I felt like I still mattered and that my condition was something others cared about. I felt acknowledged.

· <u>RESOLVE</u>'s website gives more suggestions on what we can do for those that are suffering. Of course, their suggestions are geared towards those struggling with infertility, but I think these are all great ideas for any nasty situation:

> o Send cards.

> o Let the sufferer cry on your shoulder.

> o Pray for them (and let them know you are praying for them).

> o Don't reopen any chapters in a person's life they have already closed.

Overall, people mean well. I know that I always mean well, but, just like everyone else, I mess up from time to time. It's because I don't understand. As frustrating and emotionally hard as it may be to live around others that don't get what we're after, it's something that we just have to accept as a reality.

Hopefully, as time goes on, though, more and more people will become aware of infertility and how difficult it is to live with. The more people are aware of it, the more people can begin to grasp how to best help those who are dealing with it. At least you'd think that to be true.

10

Fertile Myrtle

One look at this title and you already know where I'm going with this, don't you? But before we get there, let's really sit for a minute and think about things.

I remember when my husband and I were looking for a new (well, new to us) vehicle. We had a tight budget and could only afford so much. We had narrowed our vehicle choices down to what we knew to be safe, reliable, and within that budget. The winner ended up being a Chevy Impala. Once we knew that was for sure the car we were going to pursue, guess what happened? Chevy Impalas popped up everywhere. Suddenly everyone had one.

Not only did this happen with our car situation, but it happened with our infertility situation, too. When I desperately wanted to get pregnant, it seemed like everyone around me had to get pregnant first.

Hasn't this ever happened to you? You're searching for something, and while on the hunt, everyone else already found it? If not in any other situation, at least with when it comes to wanting a baby?

Now I don't think it's some cruel joke God wants to play on us. Rather, I just believe when we desire something so much, we have a heightened awareness of our surroundings and what we want sticks out like a sore thumb. Thus, we think it's everywhere, but with us.

Expect to See Other Pregnant Women…A Lot

When my husband and I began talking about having children, I already knew it would be a tough journey because I didn't have regular cycles at all. So, when the time came to try, I didn't wait long to go to the doctor and get some testing done. Thankfully, knowing my past history, they didn't make me wait the typical year. They did bloodwork and a HSG. Then I was put on Clomid to see how it would work. The second round on it, I was pregnant!

I tell you all of this because, for me, I didn't have to wait a full year to even get help and/or get pregnant. So, although I wanted a baby badly, there wasn't a lot of time to really notice everyone else being pregnant. However, that changed right around the time I miscarried.

A few days before we lost our baby, we had told the last of the remaining people we knew that we were with child. Go figure, right? Once we told everyone, then we lost our child. Anyway, while at this gathering, we found out two of them were pregnant. At the time, it was exciting. After miscarrying a few days later, though, my views slightly changed. One of the friends that announced their pregnancy that day had gone through a lot of treatments so I wasn't as jealous or upset about her situation. The other one, however, was able to pop out a kid whenever she wished it. You can probably guess how that made me feel.

Moving on. I mentioned to you previously about the woman at the small church I used to attend. Of course, I knew she was pregnant. I found out about her pregnancy a few weeks after we found out about ours. It was exciting that we would have children close in age that could grow up with one another. Then I miscarried and all of those hopes and dreams went down the toilet. Suddenly, I noticed she was *still* pregnant. I was not.

A few months later I got a phone call from my mother-in-law. She wanted to tell us that my husband's cousin was pregnant. Mind you, she was only 19, not married, not in any relationship, not really going anywhere with her life, didn't have a job, lived at home, wasn't going to school, etc. I think you can understand where I'm going with that. This cousin apparently decided to have a one-night stand and that's all it took for her to get what I so longingly craved for!

As time went on, this infertility support group I am a part of also, one by one, had a post from another member that was pregnant. Those women I was happy for because they were struggling like me.

This is just a few of the many examples I could give. But as you can see, those around me were getting pregnant. And this only included those I "knew". This doesn't even begin to touch the surface of those I would see on a day-to-day basis when I went out in public.

Easy Peasy Lemon Squeezy

The much larger church that I go to now has a lot of fertile people. For instance, when I had my first son, I know of at least two others that had a child within three weeks of his birth. And since I help out with the kid's ministry at church, I know there are a lot of them, and they tend to be grouped together, too. I know that the larger a church, the more kids you will have, but the more kids there are, odds are there are more fertile people around, right?

One Sunday morning when I was serving in my son's classroom, a couple other people were talking about how there were so many kids, and on top of that, there were so many currently pregnant women. I then overheard them say that there must be something in the water that they're drinking. Obviously, that's not possible, but it sort of makes sense. At least to me. I mean, what else could explain the growing numbers of women joining the preggers club?

I've also heard the phrase, "All they've got to do is look at each other and they get pregnant." Have you heard that before? I'm sure you've at least felt that way a time or two, especially if the woman is going on her second, fourth, or fifth child. Why do people say these things or even think these things?

It's because some people make getting pregnant look easy. Here we are busting our butts to just ovulate and time things correctly, hoping it'll work, and there they are just deciding it to happen and it's done. It looks like they didn't even put in any effort.

Unfortunately, when you're going through infertility, you're going to see a lot of that. Everyone will suddenly get pregnant. They'll even get pregnant with a second or third child. Pregnant women will be everywhere. All of them will seem effortless, or at least we'll assume them to be effortless.

A True Fertile Myrtle

Now I have to admit that not all the examples I shared are what we would consider a true fertile myrtle. After all, to be a fertile myrtle, you'd have to be able to get pregnant easily and often. Obviously, I shared some examples about those who also had a tough time, such as those in my infertility support group, so they wouldn't be considered fertile myrtles. But the point I was just making above was that you'll just see a lot of pregnant women so don't be surprised when you do.

I also want to mention that just because we're seeing the pregnant women everywhere and assuming they had it easy, we really don't know. We don't walk in their shoes just like they don't walk in ours. But I completely understand why it would be so easy to make that assumption.

Here are two true fertile myrtle stories, though! I don't know this family personally, but their story was shared on the local news one day. If you're interested in reading more, I have posted the link to the entire article in the back of this book.

The couple's names are Dara and Christopher Sundberg. After their fourth child, they decided that they were done so Christopher got a vasectomy. They later found out that Dara was pregnant again with their fifth child, meaning the vasectomy failed. Not wanting to take any further chances, when the fifth child was born, Dara got a tubal ligation (her tubes tied). Well, guess what? Dara got pregnant…AGAIN! This means that the vasectomy Christopher had failed twice and Dara's tubal ligation failed.

How about a family we all seem to know? You know, the Duggar family? The couple who has, I believe, at least nineteen kids? I'm pretty sure that woman has been popping out babies every year since she married. They're also always open to have more it seems. Must be nice, right? They are truly fortunate!

If those are not true fertile myrtle stories, then I'm not sure what is. Though I don't know either family, I still have to think how lucky they are. There are a lot of examples I could think of where women never had to struggle to get pregnant. Maybe some did just look at their partner or some did drink some holy water. I don't know. The bottom line is that for many women, they make getting pregnant look easy.

It's a part of life, I know. But that doesn't mean it's easy to see and deal with. It was extremely hard for me to see women get pregnant. Not so much the strangers I ran into, but at times that was difficult, too. What I want to share with you is that your feelings, if you have any (some women aren't bothered by this like I was), are understandable. Getting angry, upset, jealous, or anything else is okay as long as you don't stay there. Most importantly, what you're feeling is normal.

Ungrateful Pregnant Women

As if seeing other women pregnant when you long to be pregnant yourself wasn't bad enough, just wait until you start hearing some of the things they will say! It kind of goes with the whole territory, though. After all, if they truly had no issues getting pregnant, then they won't know what it's like to have a tough time conceiving. And if they never had a tough time conceiving, more than likely they probably take their fertility for granted. When we take things for granted we tend to be pretty naïve with our actions and especially our words.

The following things are what I have actually heard other pregnant women say, and I'm sure you have as well. Some are just annoying, but some can be very cruel when spoken in the presence of someone like you and me. All of them, though, point to someone who is ungrateful on some level.

- **"I wish I wasn't pregnant."** Maybe they say it because their pregnancy is tough on them for one reason or another. Or maybe they say it because they see something that they know they can't do or have right now. However, whatever the reason, it's a harsh thing to say, especially among the ears of someone wishing they were pregnant.

- **"I wish I didn't get pregnant."** These are just the empty words that come from the mouth of someone who is regretting the choice they made. Maybe it's just because they weren't ready to get pregnant in the first place. Who knows? What I do know is that, again, there are plenty of those who wish they were pregnant.

- **"We got pregnant the first month we tried!"** Whenever I hear a comment like this I roll my eyes and sigh. Isn't that nice that they can just do that? I mean, good for them. I just wish we all had that ability. Doesn't it seem like they are looking for a pat on the back or something? I kind of get that impression. Bottom line, though, is they don't realize just how lucky they are. And a lot of times it's these women that end of saying one of these other things.

- **"Our baby is an oops."** I'm totally guilty of saying something like that. Not about my own kids. I would never do that. I've said it about other's kids, though, but only when repeating what the parents said in the first place. The truth is, the baby may not have been wanted for one reason or another, but I don't think the baby itself is an oops. I believe all babies are precious and are a miracle from God. What I think they should say is that their actions are an oops. The baby is just a byproduct of it. Not the actual oops.

· **"I'm so fat."** This isn't a nice thing to say about yourself no matter what condition you're in, but it should, under no circumstances, be said when you're pregnant. Of course, you're getting bigger, but it's not because you're fat. You have a whole other living being growing inside of you! Something so many women long for! When women have said this, it makes me want to just slap them!

· **"I'm so uncomfortable."** This is a reasonable statement when one is with child. I mean, there's morning sickness, bloating, hemorrhoids, sore breasts, just to name a few, that you have to deal with for most of your pregnancy. I can totally understand why many women make that comment. So why did I even mention this statement? Because some women complain ALL…THE…TIME! We get it. You're miserable! But, oh, what we wouldn't give to be miserably pregnant instead of unbearably infertile.

The Cruelest Trick

The worst of all things someone could do is to claim they're pregnant when they're clearly not. Have you seen that April Fool's joke go around? I'm not a huge fan of pranks and jokes anyway, but this crosses the line. Almost every year, without fail, someone will make that joke because they think it's funny. You and I both know that it is far from it. However, because they don't understand infertility and have no experience with it whatsoever, they see no problem with their actions.

There are more statements, even actions I'm sure, that you could come up with. And they all have the power to make infertile couples cringe. Going through what we do, we'd gladly give it all up to be in their shoes. We'd take all the stretchmarks we can get. We'd gain 100 pounds. We'd puke five or more times a day if we had to. We just really want that baby! And, no, that baby would never, ever in a million years be an oops.

In closing, as you can see, there's a lot to expect from others on your infertility journey. Hopefully I've given something that can be of use to you, whether it be some tips you can implement, things you can watch out for, or just acknowledgment of everything you face. Whatever it may be, I just hope it's something.

Moving on, we'll look beyond ourselves and others, and focus more on the actual journey itself.

Part Four

***

What to Expect During the Journey

11

Decisions, Decisions, Decisions

If you didn't know by now, infertility is not usually something in which you sit around, waiting for a breakthrough. If there is no plan in place, chances are you're that much further from reaching your goal. So, what kind of plan can you put into place, and how do you go about achieving success? Examine every option carefully and follow directions to a T. Does that sound easy and doable? Well, sort of.

Expect There to Be a Lot of Options

It would be so great if there was one fix-all cure that an infertility couple could take or do that would instantly give them the baby of their dreams. But, unfortunately, that just isn't the case. There is not one simple way that works for every couple. This is why navigating through infertility can be a little tough. There are a lot of options available to infertile couples, all of which may or may not work. All options are based on what the issue is, and, of course, what the couple can afford and feels comfortable with.

What are your options? Many of these you'll already know, but for the sake of those who may not, below is a list of some ways infertility couples can make their way through their own journey:

· **Waiting.** Waiting out infertility is the easiest and cheapest way to go, yet is undoubtedly the hardest and possibly longest. Within waiting it out, you have two methods:

   o **Completely waiting it out.** In other words, doing absolutely nothing about your situation. You won't see any doctors. You won't have any tests done. You won't take any medication of any kind. You're just going to have frequent sex and hope for the best.

   o **Cycle charting.** Those who choose this path are still not taking the route of medical or natural help, but they will pay close attention to what their body may or may not be doing, and in turn, plan sex accordingly. So, these women are waiting with a twist, so to speak, because they are at least timing things in order to increase their chances of getting pregnant. They also usually keep a chart of all that is happening so they can see trends.

· **Naturally.** This is a very popular way of trying to conceive because it doesn't include any medical attention. Some people are not comfortable with medications and shots, etc., so they opt for something natural. Natural methods can also be cheaper, but, with some cases, can be riskier. There are four ways you can go about achieving pregnancy naturally:

   o **Introducing healthier habits.** The American Pregnancy Association has a list of some things that should be put into practice before getting pregnant. All of them will make for a healthier body, and in turn, will typically increase fertility. Some healthier habits include exercising, quitting smoking, limiting caffeine intake, stopping alcohol consumption, losing weight, drinking lots of water, etc.

   o **Dieting.** When I mention the word dieting, I am not referring to limiting your calories and having the goal of losing weight while eating cardboard. I am talking about incorporating the right kinds of nutrients into your eating habits so that you can be ready to carry a baby. Again, The American Pregnancy Association does a great job sharing what is the best for getting pregnant and staying pregnant.

   For example, eating a diet full of red meats can lead to endometriosis. Processed foods are full of pesticides and artificial hormones. That's just not good for anyone. On the contrary, when you eat healthy amounts of the right kind of protein, your body is able to have the correct hormone production. Eating enough fiber helps your body rid itself of toxins. Fatty acids from fish such as salmon can increase fertility. And get this: women who drank three or more glasses of whole milk per day were 70% less likely to be infertile due to lack of ovulation! The bottom line is if we eat better, not only do we feel better, but our bodies start working the way they were intended to.

o **Taking vitamins/minerals.** There are certain vitamins/minerals our bodies need to thrive. It's no wonder they play a key role in getting pregnant either. The American Pregnancy Association lists five key vitamins/minerals essential to fertility:

> § **Zinc.** Just 15 mg daily enhances fertility in both men and women.

> § **Vitamin B6.** This vitamin helps regulate estrogen and progesterone.

> § **Vitamin C.** Not only does vitamin C help trigger ovulation in women, but it helps support healthy sperm count and mobility in men.

> § **Vitamin E.** For men, vitamin E enhances sperm quality. In women, vitamin E affects hormone function.

> § **Folic Acid.** This vitamin is more for when you're pregnant because it helps support healthy fetal development. But don't wait until after you find out you're pregnant to take enough of this. Start taking the right amounts now because the earliest weeks of pregnancy are most crucial, and it's during this time that folic acid really comes into play. If you're taking a prenatal supplement, which I would highly recommend since you're trying to get pregnant, then you should be all set in the folic acid department.

The easy and nice thing about male infertility is that vitamins/minerals alone can do the trick. I already mentioned zinc. If you were to research zinc and how good it is for men, you'd be amazed! I can't say enough good things about it. According to BabyHopes.com, a fertility site that offers products as well as helpful advice on anything conception related, selenium is another great mineral for men to take as it helps with the integrity of their sperm.

o **Taking herbs.** Herbs have been around for ages. Many people see a benefit from using them. Some pieces of advice, though. If you are contemplating using herbs, you might want to see a specialist so they can have you take the right thing. You also ought to know that some herbs are dangerous while pregnant so you should probably stop taking any herbs after you ovulate so that, if you happen to get pregnant, it's out of your system. Lastly, there isn't enough proof that herbs actually help. That is, there is a lack of scientific studies. However, many, many women swear up and down by them! Here are some of the best as found on an article on BabyHopes.com that listed herbs women can take to increase fertility:

§ Evening Primrose Oil can increase the amount of cervical fluid, which helps keep sperm alive and able to enter the uterus and travel up to and through the fallopian tube.

§ Red Raspberry Leaf Extract can strengthen the uterine lining and protect any possible pregnancy.

§ Chaste Berry (Vitex) aides in regulating hormones. This is one herb I tried. I don't think that I took it long enough to see any real difference, but it did help my body eventually go through a cycle, albeit a really long one. If I would have continued or possibly taken different doses, it may or may not have worked better for me. Keep in mind those are my results. I know women who take it and it really helps!

§ Dong Quai, Black Cohosh, and False Unicorn Root also made the list due to their ability to help with regulation, toning, and pain support (as in limiting cramps and ovarian pain).

Babycenter.com provides expert advice on anything related to conceiving, to having a baby, to as the baby grows. An article they had talked about soy isoflavones, another herb women can take. Soy isoflavones is supposed to work like Clomid in that it is taken for a few days only. Once you're done taking it, your body is tricked into thinking your estrogen levels are low, and therefore, it's time to start ovulating. While this particular herb did not work for me, I know women who have used it and it worked wonders.

And since not all infertility is female-based, let's look at some things that can help men. BabyHopes.com listed these:

> § Saw Palmetto helps to stimulate the glands that produce sperm. It is also known to help with low libido and prostate issues.

> § Some herbs that may help male infertility in general include Valerian, Licorice, Red Clover, Lady's Mantle, etc. Please check out BabyHopes.com for the complete list.

There are also products out there that come as a blend of vitamins, minerals, and herbs to give optimal support. I know of two that couples have used. You get a "for her" and "for him" version, each formulated to include that which is specific to the gender. Used together, in theory, it is supposed to help couples overcome infertility. The two brands I have heard of are FertilAid and Fertility Blend. If you are interested in them, I have provided the links to their websites in the back of the book.

· **Medically.** This is the route that most couples choose to travel. It is the most expensive by far, but can be the quickest. After all, after you've done some testing and know what the root of the problem is, you know how to best address it. And with modern knowledge and technology, many times the root causes can be fixed. The only downfall is that some methods medicine uses are not comfortable to pursue for one reason or another.

Every doctor has their own way of going about achieving success. Most start with the very basic and then work up from there. Methods of achieving success will also depend on what the core problem is. Let's look at the general flow of things.

- o **Surgery.** You might be scratching your head on this one, but hear me out. If your doctor has discovered you have endometriosis or a blocked/damaged fallopian tube, most likely they'll want to perform a surgery to correct the issue. A lot of times women can then get pregnant after the surgery.

- o **Clomid.** A key reason why women can't get pregnant is due to ovulation. Clomid is a pill a woman can take to help them ovulate. Most times doctors will start on the lowest dose and work up from there. Usually six rounds is all the doctor will allow you to try.

- o **Metformin.** This is used to treat polycystic ovarian syndrome. If you and your doctor know this is something you struggle with, they will most likely prescribe you this.

- o **Hormone shots.** If Clomid didn't do the trick, the next step is hormone shots. Again, these are used to help trigger a woman to ovulate. After all, if there's no ovulation, there's no chance for pregnancy.

- o **IUI.** Now we're getting a bit more serious. A simple pill didn't work. Hormone shots aren't working. The next thing your doctor might want to try is insemination. The most popular kind is IUI (intrauterine insemination). Basically, while you're ovulating, a doctor injects your man's sperm (or a donor's sperm should you go that route) right into the uterus.

- o **IVF.** This is usually towards the end of treatments. If all else has failed to this point, you can choose to have an in-vitro fertilization performed. This is where doctors will take the woman's egg and man's sperm. If they can create a fertilized egg, they will insert it into the woman in hopes it'll stick. This process is very hard on a body and is extremely expensive.

o **Others.** There are other types of inseminations and assisted reproductive technologies that can be performed. If you ever have to get to that point, your doctor will be able to explain to you your options and what would work best in their professional opinion. WebMD did a great job listing some options based on what is going on within an infertile couple. I'd encourage you to check out their website. A link has been provided at the end of the book.

· **A Little of Everything.** It is not uncommon for many women to do a little bit of all of the above. They might be seeing their doctors, going through tests and taking certain medications, while at the same time taking extra vitamins, even some herbs, as well as eating well and cycle charting.

If You Aren't Getting Pregnant

If you are constantly seeing false pregnancy tests cycle after cycle, and have virtually gone as far as you can medically and naturally, there are still options open to you! These are not easy options by any means because it might feel like you are just giving up the hopes of having your own flesh and blood child, but they're options nonetheless.

· **Surrogacy.** This might be a strange concept to many, and I know the option is not as easily available as some others, but if you do your research, it's around. Finding someone to be a surrogate is basically allowing them to carry your child. According to WebMD, it can be done in one of the following ways:

  o **Traditionally.** This is where the surrogate would be artificially inseminated with the man's sperm. His sperm would then fertilize the surrogate's egg. After she carries and delivers the baby, she hands the baby over to you and your man. The baby would be your man's biological baby, but not yours because it was not your egg.

  o **Gestationally.** This type of surrogacy is where the surrogate carries a baby that is fully yours and fully your man's. What happens is a doctor will take your egg and your man's sperm. They'll make sure the egg gets fertilized, and then by process of in vitro fertilization, will implant the fertilized egg into the surrogate's uterus. After carrying and delivering the baby, the surrogate hands the baby over to you and your man. It's your biological child, as well as your man's biological child.

The legal process for surrogacy is tricky so it's definitely not a path many choose. But for those that do, they do get the baby they've always wanted!

I actually had a friend who called me up one day shortly after I had my miscarriage. She told me she would be my Phoebe should I need her to be. For those that do not get this reference, Phoebe was one of the characters on the hit show, Friends. In one season, Phoebe was carrying her brother's babies because her brother and his wife couldn't get pregnant. Essentially, Phoebe was being a surrogate for her brother and his wife. To know I had a friend willing to do that was a bit overwhelming at the time! But it goes to show that you don't necessarily have to go through some professional organization to do a surrogacy. Many times, family members and friends do the deed for you!

· **Fostering/Adoption.** Many people opt to go this route before even trying IUI or IVF. They figure that if they are going to pay expensive amounts on trying to have a child, they might as well use those funds for a more surefire outcome. We've already gone over some details about adoption. It's not for everyone, and, yes, it can be expensive. When at the end of all you can personally do, though, this is a way to get the baby you've always wanted. It may not be the same because there's no biological connection, but that doesn't matter. You'll still love the baby/child as if there was. And for those iffy on adoption, you could always go the fostering route first. Fostering to adopt is one of the cheaper ways to adopt, but the process is still quite lengthy and difficult at times. The awesome thing is that if you do go the route of fostering or adoption, you can always keep trying to get pregnant. The doctors may have told you your chances are slim to none, but God works miracles every day.

· **Remaining a family of two.** Some couples decide to bypass extensive measures of having a baby and remain just the two of them. Instead of spending copious amounts on adoption or IVF or any other type of procedure/path, they choose to save the money for traveling or a nicer lifestyle. Nowhere does this mean a baby isn't important to them, it's just how they best want to proceed. Of course, they'll keep trying, but they've come to the point that if it never happens, it's okay.

The bottom line is that this is your journey. There may be a billion and one ways to go about it, but it is still yours. Knowing that is true, it is up to you to figure out what you are most comfortable with, how far you want to go, and what you can reasonably afford. You need to focus on what is best for you and your partner, not on what may be popular or not so much. And, please, don't let anyone persuade or manipulate you into doing anything, or make you feel guilty for not doing something. Even if it's your doctor doing that. It's your body, your infertility, your journey. If something doesn't feel right, don't do it. If your gut tells you to try one last time, do it.

Once you have your plan in place, it's time to stick to it and follow through. Remember to take one day at a time, one step at a time since this is a process. Don't worry about if something will or will not work. Just focus on the here and now. After all, there will be a lot of waiting around and I can totally see why it would cause someone to worry or second guess things. So, I want to encourage you to breathe and remain confident. That's the only way you may stay somewhat sane.

12

What Do I Do Now?

Have you ever heard the proverbial phrase, "Patience is a virtue?" This short saying teaches us none other than the fact patience is extremely important. It's something we all need to practice on a daily basis. But is it easy? Absolutely not!

Well, guess what? If having patience is an area that you struggle with, I guarantee that going through infertility will teach you really fast. Your journey will undoubtedly make you come across many, and I mean many, opportunities in which to learn and practice patience. How? Through waiting of course!

You're already waiting on that sweet bundle of joy to enter your lives. Infertility thought it would be great if you were to wait on everything else as well. Whether it be a point in your cycle, a doctor to see you, test results to be shared, etc. You get the point.

I may never know how your infertility journey pans out. One thing I know for certain, though, is that you will come out of infertility with far more patience than you had going into it.

Expect A Lot of Waiting

I'm going to use the same transitions as I did with the sections of this book when discussing the topic of waiting. The first section was on what *you* could expect for yourself with infertility. So, I'm going to start with what will *you* be waiting on?

Everything actually all starts with you. You are the one that is trying to conceive. You are the one that has these cycles that indicate when you're most fertile and when you may or may not be pregnant. So, it makes sense to say that you will first be waiting on ovulation. In the average, regular woman's cycle, ovulation takes place roughly two weeks from when your cycle first started. That's day fourteen on the cycle chart. If you just started your period, you will need to wait about those two weeks to be at your peak fertile window.

Let's say you ovulated. Congratulations! Hopefully you knew that you were ovulating and timed sex accordingly. That definitely tips the scales in your favor for conceiving. However, the answer doesn't come the next day. You get to wait another two weeks! Some women can get accurate results shorter than the fourteen days, but most women need to wait until at least the fourteen days to see whether or not they may be pregnant.

This is true for most women. Their life will revolve around two-week cycles. Two weeks to ovulate. Two weeks to see if they're pregnant or get their period. So on and so on and so on.

What about if you're irregular? Well, then you're just waiting on anything to happen at all. That was something I had to deal with. I had no idea when I'd eventually ovulate. After I ovulated I knew I had the fourteen days before anything else would happen. But when my period would come, I had no clue when the next ovulation would occur. Often times it was five plus weeks down the road. There are others that deal with what I did. And there are other women that have it slightly worse in that they don't know when they will ovulate as well as not know when to expect the cycle to end because they are all over the place. Whatever camp you might fall into, though, regular or irregular, you're still going to experience the waiting game.

After discussing what you could expect for yourself with infertility, we looked at what you could expect from others. So, what role do others play in your wait?

I think that I could give you one word and you would nod your head, knowing full well what I'm getting at. That one word would be doctor. See what I mean? Not only will you have to wait in order to even see the doctor, but unless you have some secret I know nothing about, you will have to wait while you're at the doctor's office. I can probably count on the fingers of just one hand where I had a minimal wait. Otherwise I've had to wait extreme amounts of time for the doctor to finally knock on the door of the room I was in. It's these same doctors that you would have to wait on to perform tests, give results, and recommend what to do or where to go next. And believe me, I think they purposely make us wait sometimes, too, because there's a lot of it going on in regard to doctors alone.

Now we reached the section we are on now: what to expect about the journey. What do you think you would wait on in regard to the journey itself?

Well, you know what a get-rich-quick scheme is right? It's some kind of "business" or process that you could perform that promises tons of money overnight. All you have to do is follow those stinking rules. Have you tried any of them? Have any of them actually worked? The obvious answer is no. Why? Because if they worked, everyone would be doing it and we'd all be rich, right?

Getting pregnant is the same way. There are no get-pregnant-quick schemes that actually work. Certain people or products might swear up and down that you can get pregnant by doing a, b, and then c. However, if that were true, everyone going through infertility would try and get pregnant. Since that's not happening, we can conclude that a, b, and then c doesn't always work. So, the bottom line is that the whole journey you will embark on could be short, it could be extremely long, or it could be anywhere in between. Everyone's journey is different and varies in length. The one thing in common with every other journey is that there is at least some amount of waiting to actually get pregnant.

Let's say you decide on adoption instead of trying to conceive. You're in luck! You'll have a lot of waiting then, too! There is waiting in getting the paperwork done, the home studies completed, the actual child you want to be available and able to finally make it into your home. Sometimes there's even setbacks where you thought the child would be forever yours, only to find out something went wrong and they are now out of reach. Then it'll be time to wait some more.

The Gift of Waiting

One thing is true, in my opinion, when it comes to any path you decide to take. It's all about waiting on God to just say the word and let it happen. No amount of money, influence, power, etc., will be able to take the waiting out of infertility. It's something that just comes with the territory.

As hard as that is to believe or understand, waiting is actually a very biblical principle. I'm not going to go through every instance of waiting that is found in scripture, but in the first two books of the Bible alone we see some huge instances of waiting.

First is Abraham. In Genesis, we read that his wife, Sarah, was barren, but when he was 75 years old, God promised they would have a son. Do you know how long it took for Abraham to finally have that promised son by

Sarah? Twenty-five years! Abraham was 100 years old when Isaac was finally born. That is a long time. Perhaps it's even as long as the amount of years you've been alive! And 25 years is just from when the promise was made until it was fulfilled. Abraham and Sarah waited even longer than that if you factor in the fact they probably tried to conceive when they first were married.

A second example of waiting we see in the Bible is with Jacob. In Genesis, we see that he fell in love with Rachel hard and fast. The only problem was he had to work for her for seven years before he could marry her. When the seven years were over, he was tricked and was given Rachel's sister, Leah, instead. He was able to marry Rachel a short time later, but only at the cost of working another seven years. Now I know that some of you perhaps had a long dating or engagement experience so seven years doesn't seem that bad, but, to me, that's a long time to wait for something that was just out of reach.

The last biblical example I will share with you is from Exodus, the second book of the Bible. Right at the beginning we see God mightily delivering His people, Israel, out of Egypt. There was blood, bugs, darkness, death, and more! God's purpose of delivering Israel was so that they could go to the Promised Land. However, a trip that should have taken about eleven days ended up taking 40 years. I repeat, 40 years! If that's not waiting a long time, I don't know what is.

Why do you think God asks us to wait? Or, rather, not just ask, but actually has us wait? An article by Vaneetha Rendall Risner titled "The Unwelcome Gift of Waiting" gives such a beautiful response. The specific answer will be different for every single one of us. But generally, "Waiting is not just about what I get at the end of the wait, but about who I become as I wait." Basically, waiting teaches us to cling to Him rather than to a certain outcome. This will further increase our faith and prepare us for how He wants to use us. Waiting actually has a purpose!

I know that answer may not be a welcome piece of information. I know that waiting is not popular and many people associate waiting with God choosing to ignore us and what we most desire. That's okay if that's you. Everyone has their own opinion. However, this is simply just a truth that I see for myself, as well as one I have seen in the lives of many others.

Passing Time

The same article I listed above, "The Unwelcome Gift of Waiting," said it best: "It's hardest to wait when I am uncertain about the outcome." Unless you can see the future, you have no clue how your infertility journey will come to a close and a new chapter in your life will open. Through this uncertainty, it's easy to get worried, depressed, doubtful, and so on and so on. So, what I would like to do is provide some ideas on ways you can pass your time, some of which were taken from RESOLVE's website. It's not so that you stay so busy that you don't even have time to breathe. Rather, these ideas are to offer an outlet so you can stay in somewhat control of your sanity as well as maintain some small amount of joy in living. After all, anything is better than sitting around twiddling your thumbs, right?

· **Binge watch your favorite show.** I wouldn't recommend being totally lazy and constantly shutting yourself in to binge watch something on Netflix, Hulu, or the like. However, on occasion, this is an excellent way to get your time to go slightly faster. If you don't have a favorite show, there are tons of options out there that you could find yourself getting addicted to. Add on some comfy clothes and yummy snacks and you've got yourself a night of enjoyment.

· **Read.** We all know that reading a good book can transport our minds to another world, which is where you probably wish you were about now. So, what you could do is take some time to find some books in a genre you love most and read.

· **Go on a mini-vacation.** Not everyone can afford this or see the point in this, but the purpose of a mini-vacation would be to relax, get away from home, and enjoy what's out there. You don't necessarily have to go far, and you don't have to go for long, hence the phrase mini-vacation. An example, my husband and I love to go up north. Living in Western Michigan, that means anything north of Big Rapids. Specifically, we love the Gaylord, Michigan, area. It's about three hours north of where we live. So, some weekends we choose to go there. We don't do a whole lot. It's just to relax and get away from everything that's going on at home.

· **Take up a hobby.** If you do anything with Pinterest, you already have a clue as to the many things you could start doing. Some ideas are scrapbooking, decorating, knitting, recipe trying, etc. You never know what you might start enjoying.

· **Write.** This is something you could do privately, such as keeping a journal, or something you could do publicly, such as a blog, if you're comfortable with it. If you really like to write, you could do both. Writing helps people process the feelings they have, as well as helps put into words everything they are going through.

· **Do a special date night.** Date nights are something that all couples should do at least once in a while. However, sometimes you just need to sneak an extra one in. Whether you've just gotten bad news, or you're stressed over something coming up, or anything else, a special time carved out with your partner might do the trick to help you feel better. I know it always did for me. And if you don't have tons of money, a special date night doesn't have to be anything expensive. You could just go to the park or beach and walk if you wanted to.

· **Try something new.** Doing something different and new can add a slight thrill. Maybe you could take a painting class or try some dancing lessons. If you like sports, maybe you could go miniature golfing, roller skating, or even ice skating. Join a league of some sort. Options are almost endless.

· **Make letters for your future baby.** Some people want to stay super positive while they wait for their baby to arrive. One way they do that is by writing letters to their future baby. You could share how much your baby is wanted and loved. You could share some things you had to go through to get your baby. Whatever is on your heart to let your baby know, write it down to them.

· **Garden.** People associate gardening with fertility. As you plant seeds and watch them grow, it's like getting pregnant and having your baby. Planting a garden and caring for it can provide a lot of healing therapy to an individual.

· **Gather the girls.** When you really need some time to hang loose and have some fun, gather up all your closest friends for a girl's night. Do something simple, formal, or downright wild and crazy. These times can bring a lot of laughter and definitely some good memories.

· **Relax at the spa.** This is not my cup of tea, but there are many women out there that love to go to the local spa and get a massage, or depending on what the spa all offers, they get a manicure, pedicure, new hairstyle, etc. It's all about being pampered. With all you're going through, you do deserve some pampering!

Like I mentioned before, the purpose of passing your time is not so that you stay ridiculously busy. I am not trying to get you to ignore what you're going through or forget your troubles, although I'm sure at times that sounds like a good plan. All that I'm encouraging is for you to find some ways that you can pass your time that will keep you healthy, happy, hopeful, and, maybe most importantly, sane.

13

Testing, Testing, 1, 2, 3

When you were in school, were you good at taking tests? Did you like taking tests in the first place? If so, you're going to love what this chapter is about. If, on the other hand, you're not so good at taking tests, and, frankly, you're like most people and would rather not have tests at all, then I'm afraid I've got some bad news.

Expect A Lot of Testing

If you thought tests were something that just happened while in school and that you should be long done with them by now, you're in for a huge surprise. Life in general is a string of tests, all of which help improve our character and make us stand stronger.

Infertility, in and of itself, is a huge test. But within that monstrous test, you'll find many, many, tiny tests (not that the tests themselves are insignificant; they're just not as big as the overall picture). Some of these tests might be easy to pass. Others, not so much. Let's examine some ways in which you will be tested.

· **Physical testing.** These kinds of tests are any of them that require the body. It might be a test you take or one that is performed on you. Some you can do alone. Others are by the professionals. While some tests will be over quickly and painlessly, some will require time and a little bit of discomfort. What are some examples? I'm glad you asked!

  o **Ovulation tests.** Not all women choose to take ovulation tests. I don't blame them. They can be pricey, and each cycle you probably will have to take at least a few to see the results you're looking for. If you do take these tests, hopefully this is one you pass each and every cycle.

  o **Pregnancy tests.** This is the type of test we're all longing to pass, right? Most women that go through infertility end up taking a pregnancy test almost each and every cycle. Although the most accurate ones are expensive, you can buy some cheaper ones in bulk that generally work just as good.

o **Bloodwork.** If you have troubles getting pregnant, your doctor will for sure have all kinds of bloodwork done on you. Hormones and other chemicals in the body, if not working properly, throw a woman's body off so a doctor orders a complete work up to see if they can pin point the culprit. And because your bloodwork changes all the time, your doctor may have repeat tests done at different times during your cycle. Depending on whether you like needles or not, these tests could be uncomfortable. You also usually have to wait at least a few days before you know any concrete results.

o **HSG.** Thankfully this is a test that only needs to be performed once. The purpose is to see if your tubes are blocked. The doctor performing this test inserts a dye through the cervix, and while watching a screen, can see if the dye makes it through each of the fallopian tubes. The test is quick, but can be very uncomfortable. My doctor even recommended I take some aspirin before getting the test done.

As a side note, perhaps something that's funny, I did a HSG towards the beginning of my infertility journey. Right when the dye was inserted, my husband exclaimed, "Oh, that's cool!" Now I'm sure it looked neat on the screen he and the doctor were watching, but all I kept thinking was if it was so cool, he should be getting this test done. Obviously, that isn't possible, but you would not have wanted to see my face just then.

o **Post-coital test.** This is an examination that requires having sex first. Once your man has deposited his sperm into the vagina, the doctor will check to see how well the sperm and cervical mucous interact.

o **Ultrasounds.** These are usually performed when a doctor wants to check the internal reproductive organs to make sure they're all there and that there's no cysts or abnormalities. Then, of course, you will get ultrasounds should you become pregnant as well.

   o **Semen analysis.** Men get the long end of the stick here. They're so lucky! While women have to be poked and prodded in every which way over every part of our goods, men just have to make love to a cup. That's it! Once their swimmers are in the container, the lab examines the quantity and quality of the sperm. Again, usually there's at least a few days of waiting before you hear the results.

· **Emotional testing.** Remember that whole chapter where I discussed infertility will bring you on an emotional rollercoaster? Well, all of those ups and downs are because you'll go through situations (tests, if you will) that set you off. You could be doing super well emotionally, going about your business. And then BAM! Out from nowhere you're hit by a train (figurative one obviously). Suddenly your emotions change. What happened?

   o You found out your best friend is pregnant…again!

   o Someone asked you a stupid question regarding your journey.

   o Your sister just had her baby.

   o You went to the store and, apparently, it was pregnant-women-unite day.

   o The pregnancy test was negative.

   o Your period showed up slightly early.

   o Insert your own "train" here.

Whatever is going on, the main thing is that all these little situations are testing your emotions, your coping capabilities, your sanity.

· **Relational testing.** Infertility can and will put a strain on many of your relationships. It is essentially testing to see if the relationship can last.

You may find these relationships being tested in your life:

o **With you partner.** This is probably one of the biggest relationships that is tested, if not the biggest one. It's easy to not agree on a path to take. No two people cope with situations the same. Desires and motivations change and even fade. Sex isn't what it used to be. All of these things and more can put a bind in a marriage. Like I've mentioned before, many couples have even divorced over this. So, yeah, to say your relationship with your partner is tested is an understatement.

o **With family and/or friends.** These people might be the ones saying the wrong things, or perhaps they just aren't supporting you the way you think they should be. There will probably even be family and friends that get to have their babies while you have to wait. That can make it hard. Especially if you're expected to be at certain celebrations or to act a certain way at those events, it can ruin the bond you have with your family and/or friends.

o **With pregnant women in general.** Whether you know them or not, when you see a pregnant woman, it could potentially evoke feelings in you. It could be happiness and longing, but it could also be bitterness, jealousy, or even discontentment. It's super easy to go from seeing them as just another human being, to seeing them as she who has what I want. Sometimes they can even become targets of our facial expressions, be it good or bad ones.

o **With doctors.** It's easy to wonder if our doctors are really doing all they can for us. It's easy to accuse them of not caring, thinking they see us as just another patient, a paycheck even. We might even question their methods or reasoning behind certain directions they want to take.

o **With God.** For those that do have a relationship with God, it'll probably be tested just as much as your relationship with your partner is tested. Why? Because we're not getting what we think we deserve. Because we're upset that God's timing isn't now like we want it to be. Because if God is in control, why doesn't He just make us pregnant? Or because if God is so good, why are we suffering? These concepts cause many Christian women to struggle with their faith during infertility. Some of these women learn to cling closer to God, but others just get mad at Him, and a few stop believing in Him all together.

Speaking of God, there is one last type of testing that infertility will put you through. However, because there's so much that needs to be said in regard to it, I figured it should be its very own section.

Spiritual Testing

Before I dig any further into some biblical stuff, I want to make a side note. Some of you reading this may not believe in God or the Bible. Or you may just be in a place where you can't allow yourself to believe what I'm about to share with you to be true. Whatever your feelings are in regard to God and His word, if you feel it's best to skip this part of the chapter, that's okay. The only reason I am sharing the following information with you is because it is something I came to terms with as truths in my own life. I am in no way trying to pressure you into believing what I do. This is just simply something I found to be helpful when walking my infertility journey.

I'm going to start with a Bible verse. James 1:2-4 says, "Dear brothers and sisters, when troubles of any kind come your way, consider it an opportunity for great joy. For you know that when your faith is tested, your endurance has a chance to grow. So, let it grow, for when your endurance is fully developed, you will be perfect and complete, needing nothing." As hard as it might be to find our troubles, namely infertility, a great joy, there is a purpose behind it.

Before we discover what that may be, I want to share some examples from the Bible itself of those who have been tested.

· In Genesis 22, we again find Abraham a key part of the story. We already know that he had to wait 25 years to get the promised son that he and his wife, Sarah, longed for. In this chapter, we are at a time after Isaac had been born, and God asks Abraham to go up a mountain and sacrifice him. Why would God ask Abraham to sacrifice his promised son? Because He is testing Abraham's faith and obedience. And you know what? Isaac ends up surviving because God provided a ram to be sacrificed instead. However, if God hadn't provided that ram, Abraham knew beyond a shadow of a doubt that God would have somehow made things okay in the end because Isaac was his promised son and God always keeps His promises.

· The Israelites are all descendants of Abraham through Isaac. When God miraculously delivered them out of Egypt, there were many times God had tested them to see where their allegiance lied, as well as if they'd be obedient. In the book of Exodus, we see God testing the Israelites in regard to water and food. Being in the desert, there was a lack of them both. God even used the surrounding nations that had yet to be driven out from the Israelites' land as a test (Judges 2:21-22). The Israelites failed many times, causing a lot of heartache, and in some cases, a lot of death.

· Job is an interesting person. No one is one hundred percent sure as to where his story fits in. Many think he was alive around the time of Abraham, but he could have been alive much earlier or even later. However, his story is important enough to have a whole book on it! If you don't know what he went through, I'd encourage you to read the book of Job. He lost his children, his wealth, and even his health. His friends even gave awful advice, basically saying it all happened because he was a horrible sinner. I'm not going to lie: Job had moments of questioning and said some things he shouldn't have. He, of course, didn't understand why everything was happening, much like we don't today. But he never stopped believing in God. When he had endured his testing, God had blessed him with more than he had at the beginning!

One unique thing about Job's testing that I find interesting is that Satan had to go before God and ask for it to happen. He can't do anything without God permitting him to. To me, it was comforting to know God has the upper hand.

· God's own son, Jesus, also had to go through some testing. After He was baptized, he fasted for forty days and forty nights. To say He was hungry wouldn't quite cut it. Anyway, Satan used this time to try and tempt Jesus to succumb to him. Three times Satan offered different things. All three times Jesus would have none of it. I'm sure that being the Son of God helped Him to fight off each and every test, but the point is He was still tested.

As you can see, testing happens to us all. It happened from the beginning of time and continues to take place today. No matter who you are, life will test you in some way from time to time. No one can escape it. The only question that now remains is why?

First of all, it's not because God is a mean, tyrannical being that finds enjoyment in creating tests for us to walk through. He doesn't use them to punish us, or, worse yet, kill us. To find out why God allows tests to be placed along our paths, we need to not so much look at the test itself and instead look at the person the test is being done to. The purpose behind testing has to deal with changing the person.

All testing of any degree is to see where our faith and obedience lie. If any of that is not where it should be, it needs to change. To change it, God tests it. It's His way of creating us into who He wants us to truly be. When we're the best us we can be, we glorify God.

Basically, God desires ultimate holiness over complete happiness. What does that even mean? It certainly doesn't mean He doesn't want us to be happy. It just means that God would rather we be holy like Him (an inside change) than happy because of an outside change. That might sound really odd or even harsh, but it's actually a really good thing.

To help you understand what I'm getting at, look at these ways God sharpens us (makes us holier) through infertility (a test). Some are ideas from Scary Mommy's website, a place where many moms unite with one common theme: parenting doesn't have to be easy, in their article titled "10 Ways Infertility Before Parenthood Changes You". Others are character attributes that are bound to shine in moments of extreme testing.

· **Patience.** All of the waiting and longing to get what you most desire will inevitably produce patience. This character trait comes in super handy if you do end up having kids. If you don't, it still comes in handy when dealing with other people, especially co-workers, your partner, and even someone like the new cashier at the grocery store who's going as slow as molasses.

· **We'll no longer take things for granted.** I often think of this truth
   when I look at my kids. I'm not saying that all people who had no
   experience with infertility take their kids for granted, but those who
   do go through infertility first tend to have this deeper gratitude for
   what they have. They know how special their children are, and that
   they're truly a gift. If you don't end up having children, there are
   other things you'll learn to never take for granted again. Any miracle
   will be seen through new eyes; will be appreciated deeper.

· **Unfairness will resonate deeper.** What this means is that you know
   that life isn't always fair. Therefore, you act in a manner that is
   sensitive. You're more conscious on how you go about doing your
   thing, knowing full well that others may not be as lucky as you. And
   I'm not just talking about if you were to get pregnant. It could be with
   something as simple as a bonus or promotion at work. It could be that
   you're able to vacation all the time when most normal people can't.
   The bottom line is that you're more aware of life's unfairness, and so
   you live in a way that is sensitive to all life around you.

· **Compassion.** Infertility will definitely give you a greater compassion
   for all the hurt in the world. It could be you see someone crying, and
   instead of ignoring it, you comfort them. After all, I'm sure you can
   remember all the times you've cried. When people are hurting, you
   care deeply because you know what it's like to hurt.

· **Sins against children will anger you.** You know that children are a
   miracle, and that they don't just come whenever we please. They
   don't grow on trees! Knowing how precious they are, seeing bad
   things happen to them will raise a righteous anger within you.
   Whether it's human trafficking, kidnapping, child abuse, or whatever
   else, you will never understand how someone could do that to an
   innocent child. Many times, the anger bubbles over until you do
   something about it.

· **You'll appreciate children more.** Going through infertility makes you
   constantly aware of the fact children are a miracle; a gift to be highly
   treasured. The bond you have with your own future children (if you

have any) or children in general will be stronger. You'll be able to accept certain behaviors when many might be quick to punish or be unable to handle them.

· **Love.** Those who never went through infertility before love their children. But I truly think that if you've gone through infertility first, your love is deeper, stronger. If you never end up having children, you still know how to love in ways the average person doesn't.

Have you seen any of these changes welling up in you yet? You don't have to have children to notice them.

Obedience Over Understanding

The thing with spiritual testing is that it is so hard to understand. We don't get why it has to happen to us and why now. With infertility, for example, we might ask why can't it be the teenage girl having one-night stands? Why am I having trouble now when I've already had a child or two before? Why can't I have some other test to endure instead? All of these may be great questions to ask, and maybe someday we'll figure out the answer. But these questions miss the point.

God doesn't need us to understand. He doesn't even need us to approve the testing. He just needs us to accept it and to fully obey Him. Let me put it in layman's terms by using an example. Think about when a parent asks a child to do something. It could be something like cleaning up after themselves. A child, especially a young one, won't understand why they're asked to do that. They'll probably put up a fight, complain, dilly dally, etc. It's because they just don't get the fact that cleaning up after themselves teaches responsibility, tidiness, and let's not forget, could prevent something from getting lost, broken, or someone getting hurt. Those ideas are too large for their minds to comprehend. But the parents of that child never asked for them to understand the concept. They only asked them to clean up after themselves, and fully expected them to obey.

It's the same way with God. He knows our finite minds will not understand why we've been chosen to go through infertility. He's only asking us to accept what we've been dealt, and to fully obey Him through it.

I want to share a piece of my journey that corresponds to this lesson of testing that I learned. After we had our miscarriage, as soon as we were able to try again, we did. We went back to the doctor and started back on the treatment plan we were previously on before we got pregnant. My first thought was that it wouldn't take long to get pregnant again. After all, it worked before so it should work now, right?

After a couple rounds, I was getting nowhere. There was even a round I didn't even ovulate. We were at the very beginning of talks about moving up to the next step, which would have been shots. I hate shots and was not thrilled with that, but kept that information in the back of my head as something I might have to endure.

During this same time, though, I've heard of other women having some success with different natural methods like with herbs and such. So, when one more round of Clomid got me nowhere yet again, my husband and I made the decision to try the natural route. Our doctor was okay with that and basically let us know that should we need to come back in to try medicine again to just give him a call. I thought that was pretty cool.

Anyway, I tried soy isoflavones first. I was getting nowhere on that so I tried Vitex next. It kind of did the trick, but not well enough or quick enough. I felt like I had just wasted months by going the natural route. However, many find success this way so please don't alter anything based on my story alone. Wanting to go back to the doctor, I called him up and scheduled to see him as soon as I could.

The doctor, my husband, and I decided to go on Clomid first. This time I was at the highest dose they like to use. I begged God to let it work. I didn't want to have to do the shots. You know the answer I got instead? To stop it all! That's right. In the midst of my infertility test, God was testing me even further. I just kept clearly feeling that I needed to stop all kinds of treatment all together and trust Him to make it work.

I did NOT like this. I wholeheartedly believed that if I were to stop treatments that I'd never get pregnant, and that was exactly the opposite of what I wanted. I did not understand why God was asking me to do this. I wrestled and tried to compromise, but it always ended up being to stop. So, in 2008 we stopped trying. Well, we still had sex all the time, but stopped using medicines or herbs. I'm so glad my husband was super supportive, because had he not been, I'm not sure I would have followed through with what I felt God calling me to do.

Do you think I got pregnant right away? No! It was over two years later before I actually found out I was pregnant with my oldest son. Was that two years of waiting, basically doing nothing, easy? Far from it. Many times, I thought about going back to the doctor or trying another herb that sounded promising. Yet, I didn't. I'm so thankful God pulled me through that test. I know that all of those areas mentioned above where we may be sharpened are definitely areas in which I changed for the better. By clinging to God, I allowed Him to make me holier through this trial. Had I not gone through infertility, I would have been happy getting what I wanted, but I'm almost certain my character would have been worse off, and my faith in God would definitely have not been where it is today.

This is just my story. I am by no means bragging or declaring I'm better than you, or holier than you, or more blessed than you, or anything among those lines. Please don't misconstrue any part of what I shared to mean any of that. I am also not saying that going beyond Clomid or anything else is wrong. This is just my story and what God called me to do. It's going to be different for every single woman. I'm also not promising that certain things will produce certain outcomes. Why? Because, again, this is just what happened for me. Your story and your results will be different than mine. The only reason I shared this with you is for an example of obeying over understanding. It is also an example of holiness over happiness. So please don't take it to mean more than that.

A Reward

I want to end this chapter on a positive note. James 1:12 says, "God blesses those who patiently endure testing and temptation. Afterward they will receive the crown of life that God has promised to those who love him."

That's great news, right? If you endure your test, you will be blessed. Now don't take this to mean that you'll get a baby out of it. I hope that you do! But, unfortunately, not all couples that go through infertility end up with a baby at some point. However, somehow and in some way, you will be blessed. It might be in your marriage. It could be with your finances. It could be a million different things. And, yet, it could be none of them, meaning your reward won't be in this day and age. One thing is for sure, though. In the end, when this life is said and done, you'll receive the crown of life! Meaning, you'll be crowned as a princess, and will live forever with our King in heaven!

In closing this chapter, I completely understand the idea of testing is not a popular or fun one. If you struggle with this concept, know that most of us do. I hope in some way, though, I've either shined a new light on it, or inspired you with it, or at least something. I guess what I really hope you gleaned from this chapter is that there is a purpose behind what you're going through. Be patient with it, endure it, and you will be blessed.

14

No Pain, No Gain

With almost everything, if we want to gain something, there tends to be at least a little bit of pain. Thus, the phrase that makes up the title of this chapter has been coined. Infertility is no exception. It doesn't just cause a little bit of pain. It causes a lot of pain in many ways on every level. But it can also provide a way to receive the greatest gain, and I don't mean just by having babies! In the meantime, though, it won't be easy.

Expect It to Feel Like Hell

Okay, okay, okay. Technically no one knows what hell is really like. No one has successfully been there and made it back to inform the rest of us. However, we do know that it is a place of extreme suffering that never quits. We also know that it is a place where God is not. With all the physical, emotional, relational, and spiritual pain that is associated with infertility, it's no small wonder why women are quick to compare it to hell. And, I might add, there's absolutely no way to get around it. Infertility is what it is.

Just like I've done previously, I'm going to briefly discuss the suffering infertility couples experience by dividing it all into groups.

- **Physical suffering.** This one is probably not hard to imagine. Tests that you take can be painful, especially when they have anything to do with your insides. Side effects from medicines and herbs can be unbearable at times. Clomid, for example, can cause some nasty headaches. I should know, seeing as I was the recipient of many of them. You should also expect hot flashes with Clomid. And that's just a couple side effects from just one drug. Other treatments, natural or medical, can cause all sorts of pain and uncomfortableness. There are even women that deal with infertility where their very own periods are downright painful.

- **Emotional suffering.** When your mind plays tricks on you and your emotions take you from high to low and around the block five times, it can be a living nightmare. Your emotions can and will make things tough on you as well as on those around you.

· **Relational suffering.** When couples deal with infertility, there are often broken relationships. Sometimes it's with each other, but many times it's with those they thought they were close with such as friends and family. When you're in a place where you need to keep yourself from certain events, there's isolation. It can be torture to many women to have a disruption in the relationships they have.

· **Spiritual suffering.** For some people, this can sometimes be the hardest suffering to deal with because the God we thought we knew to be one who protects, provides, and grants good things is now seen as one who has abandoned us, is punishing us, or no longer loves us. In essence, we feel He is silent when He should be speaking up loud and clear. While these thoughts and feelings couldn't be further from the truth, we still feel attacked and are left wondering why we must go through what we're going through. We beg God to answer us when we ask why we have to suffer.

Suffering's Purpose

Before I actually delve into suffering's purpose, there are two things I want to share with you. The first is that what you are about to read will sound a lot like what you've read in the past chapter. While the basic principles of testing and suffering are close in nature, they are still separate. Testing is what we're going through, while suffering is what we feel when going through the testing. Therefore, I opted to speak on each subject separately instead of on them collectively. If you find it all redundant, it's okay. Like I said, there will be a lot of the same themes.

The second thing I want to say is that, as you may have guessed, what is coming is again of a Christian view point. These are things that I found to be inspirational to my infertility journey. They are truths that I clung to, and still do today. If God, or the Bible, or anything Christian related is not your cup of tea, feel free to move on to the next chapter. I know that, to many people, what I'm about to share is a foreign concept. It isn't easily understood nor something that people are greatly fond of. And that's okay. I'm only sharing because I found it helpful, and I'm hoping that at least one other person will find this information helpful as well.

Okay. That said, let's move on to suffering's purpose. Internationally known mouth artist, vocalist, radio host, author, and advocate for disabled persons, Joni Eareckson Tada, was in a diving accident that left her a quadriplegic in 1967. To read her full story, please check out her website that I have listed in the back of this book. She once said, "God permits what He hates to accomplish what He loves."

Let's dissect what she's saying.

· The first thing she said was, "God permits." What this means is that God is not punishing you with infertility. He's not a mean God who likes to inflict suffering on you, and He's not trying to pay you back for something that you did. Don't get me wrong. Sometimes we do have to face the consequences of our sin. However, most of the stuff we suffer with are not because of our sin. They are because we live in a fallen world. Living in a fallen world means there is a lot of pain. That pain is bound to inflict us at some point in some way.

To prove that point, I want to share two Bible verses with you. The first is Luke 13:1-5. It says, "About this time Jesus was informed that Pilate had murdered some people from Galilee as they were offering sacrifices at the Temple. "Do you think those Galileans were worse sinners than all the other people from Galilee?" Jesus asked. "Is that why they suffered? Not at all! And you will perish, too, unless you repent of your sins and turn to God. And what about the eighteen people who died when the tower of Siloam fell on them? Were they the worst sinners in Jerusalem? No, and I tell you again that unless you repent, you will perish, too.""

The second Bible verse is found in John 9:1-3. The verses say, "As Jesus was walking along, he saw a man who had been blind from birth. "Rabbi," his disciples asked him, "Why was this man born blind? Was it because of his own sins or his parents' sins?" "It was not because of his sins or his parents' sins," Jesus answered. "This happened so the power of God could be seen in him.""

Bad things don't necessarily happen because we're sinners or because of a particular sin we committed in general. Bad things happen because we live in a fallen world. My husband and I had two very different viewpoints on this. When I had my miscarriage, he took the blame. He truly felt that we lost that baby because of some sins from his past. I, on the other hand, lovingly reassured him that's not true (even though I, too, questioned if my own sin had something to do with it). Yes, God does sometimes allow bad things to happen because of a sin we commit. I mean, consequences are only to be expected. But that doesn't mean every single occurrence of suffering is directly related to a particular thing we did wrong. If you aren't convinced, read and reread those two Bible verses I just shared.

Going back to the original phrase, remember, "God permits." This means He's allowing it to happen, not causing it to happen. He's allowing infertility to be a part of your life, not causing it to because of what you or your partner did or didn't do.

· The second part of her phrase is, "What He hates." God HATES infertility. Do you want to know how I know that? Because He can't contradict Himself. If He wants us to be fruitful and to multiply (Genesis 1:28), if He seeks godly children from the union we have with our partner (Malachi 2:15), He can't then turn around and like infertility. Infertility is the exact opposite of what God desires.

God also hates the fact that bad things happen in general. I know that because God loves us so much that He sacrificed His own son for us (John 3:16). Loving someone that much means you would never want them to experience pain and suffering. So why have suffering at all then?

· "To accomplish what He loves." This final phrase explains quite a bit if we just think about it. Just like what I shared in the last chapter, God might be trying to accomplish a better character, or more faithfulness, compassion, patience, etc., in you. Anything that makes us holier people is what He loves. So, whatever you're going through, be it infertility or any other type of suffering, it is being permitted to accomplish something in you.

We may never know what that is, but we know it's for our good.

Romans 8:28 says, "And we know that God causes everything to work together for the good of those who love God and are called according to his purpose for them." I know it sounds weird to say that going through infertility is for our good, and by no means does it feel good, but it's definitely the method God is choosing to allow to happen for our good. Whatever that good may be.

Suffering's Best Example

I can think of no better example of suffering than in Jesus Christ Himself. Though He is the Son of God, He came to this fallen earth as a human. You would think He could be born in the best of places under the best of circumstances, but He wasn't. He was born in a dirty manger, surrounded by animals. The king at the time, King Herod, sought to destroy Him.

As He grew and became a man, it would be reasonable to think He would have lived well off, being rich and well-liked. Not so. He wandered from place to place to place, many people still seeking to destroy Him.

Then it all comes to a head at a young age. Barely into His thirties and His life is cut short. Jesus was betrayed by a close friend. When He had been brought before different leaders and the sentence was death, He was severely beaten. Matthew 27:26-31 says, "So Pilate released Barabbas to them. He ordered Jesus flogged with a lead-tipped whip, then turned Him over to the Roman soldiers to be crucified. Some of the governor's soldiers took Jesus into their headquarters and called out the entire regiment. They stripped Him and put a scarlet robe on Him. They wove thorn branches into a crown and put it on His head, and they placed a reed stick in His right hand as a scepter. Then they knelt before Him in mockery and taunted, "Hail! King of the Jews!" And they spit on Him and grabbed the stick and struck Him on the head with it. When they were finally tired of mocking Him, they took off the robe and put His own clothes on Him again. Then they led Him away to be crucified."

That doesn't sound like a walk in the park, does it? Remember, Jesus deserved none of this. He didn't do a single thing that would have or should have caused Him to die. Yet, there He goes through all the torture and ridicule. Eventually they nail Him to a cross where He pretty much had to endure a slow, painful death.

Could He have avoided this? Yes. He is God after all. Did He even want to go through all of this in the first place? This might be surprising to some, but no. Jesus did NOT want to go through suffering and death. Matthew 26:39 clearly states, "He went on a little farther and bowed with His face to the ground, praying, "My Father! If it is possible, let this cup of suffering be taken away from me. Yet I want your will to be done, not mine."" You see, Jesus didn't want to suffer, especially when He knew what was coming.

But He did it. He obediently went through all that He needed to go through. Why? Because of His love for us. What's more, His suffering was for His good, as well as for our good. Salvation would never be possible if Jesus would have decided to walk away from the cross.

Putting It All Together

Probably having already exhausted the subject of testing and suffering, let me leave you with a few things:

- **Suffering is common.** It happens to everyone in one way, shape, or form. It's also normal. So, do not feel that what you are experiencing is new, rare, or so unique that you're all alone in the world.

- **No suffering is put to waste.** What I mean by that is there is always some kind of good result that comes from suffering. That good result is going to be different for every single person, but the bottom line is that every single person will get a good result. Never has anyone suffered just because.

- **The greatest suffering always produces the greatest beauty.** Ecclesiastes 3:11 says, "Yet God has made everything beautiful for its own time. He has planted eternity in the human heart, but even so, people cannot see the whole scope of God's work from beginning to end." In the example of Jesus, He suffered much. I don't think anyone has or ever will suffer as much as He did. But it also produced the greatest beauty, which is the salvation of all of those who put their trust in Him. We can't see all God has in mind from beginning to end when it comes to our infertility, but in its time, it will produce something beautiful. Your story will end up being a work of art.

Having said all of that, I know that these words and thoughts can be hard to read and difficult to understand. If you're in a place where you can't believe them, that's okay. It's normal to struggle with these concepts. I sure did, and still do on occasion. Each person comes to grips with this in their own timing and in their own way, if at all. It's a decision everyone makes for themselves. The only reason I have shared it is because it is something I've learned. Whether you agree or not, I hope you have still been able to see another viewpoint on all you're going through.

Part Five

***

What to Remember About the Journey

15

Tale as Old as Time

The first thing we need to remember in regard to our infertility journey is that this is not something new. Yes, it's new to you because you've never gone through it before (unless you're experiencing secondary infertility after having experienced primary infertility). But infertility, the disease itself, is not new. Almost since the beginning of the world, there have been women (and their partners) who have had troubles conceiving. Come travel time with me as we look at infertility through the ages.

Bible Times

For those of you, like me, who believe the Bible is God's written word, and is true down to every last character, you'll find actual examples of women who were barren. Not every disease known to mankind has the opportunity to showcase itself in the Bible, so the fact infertility does not just once, but seven times, is pretty significant.

· To find our first example, you don't have to look further than the beginning of Genesis. In Genesis Chapter 15, God promises Abraham that his descendants will be as numerous as the stars in the sky. That sounds far-fetched to just about anyone, but to someone who was older and had yet had any children at all because his wife, Sarah, was unable to become pregnant (Genesis 11:30), it sounds like something way out in the left field of the ballpark.

Despite that, however, Abraham believed what God had told him. Sometime later, seeing as she still didn't have children, Sarah allowed her husband to have her maidservant. If her maidservant got pregnant, the descendants could come through that child. Although God allowed Sarah's maidservant to, in fact, get pregnant, that was not the promised child He was referring to.

In Genesis Chapter 17, we see God, once again, declaring His promise that Sarah would have a son. This time Abraham laughed. Why? Because he was 100 years old and Sarah was 90! People today hardly make it to this age. If we did, though, we'd probably laugh, too, had God told us that's when we'd have a baby. Genesis 18:11 even confirms the ridiculousness of the claim because it says that Sarah was well past the age of having children. And yet, "Is anything too hard for the Lord" (Genesis 18:14)? Nope! In Genesis 21, we read that exactly when God said it would happen, Isaac was born. Isaac was the long-awaited child that would come from Abraham AND Sarah. Imagine that! A son to a very old couple who could not get pregnant.

· Not much is written about Rebekah, Isaac's wife. Then again, not a whole lot is said about him either. But we do know at least one thing: they struggled to get pregnant. In Genesis 25:21, "Isaac pleaded with the Lord on behalf of his wife because she was unable to have children." No one knows how long it took for that pleading to take place and when God finally obliged, but the point is He did. Rebekah ended up getting pregnant with twins.

· The next woman from the Bible to have struggled with infertility is Rachel. She is one of the wives of Jacob, one of Rebekah's twins. Not only did she have to live with the fact her father deceived her and Jacob, allowing Rachel's older sister, Leah, to get married to Jacob first, but she had to live with the fact her sister could spit out kid after kid after kid when she couldn't. And it was all because Leah was unloved. Genesis 29:31 says, "When the Lord saw that Leah was unloved, he enabled her to have children, but Rachel could not conceive." The Bible goes on to say that Rachel got very jealous, and she and Jacob had a very heated debate over it. Finally, after maidservants were given to Jacob and more children were born, "God remembered Rachel's plight and answered her prayers by enabling her to have children" (Genesis 30:22). Rachel only ended up having two sons, dying right after her second son was born.

· Many years later, when Abraham's descendants were getting to be as many as the stars in the sky, we see another couple struggling to have a baby. We only know the man's name, which is Manoah, and the fact his wife was not able to get pregnant (Judges 13:2). However, after

the Lord appears to them, letting them know they will indeed have a
son, that precious baby boy was born. You may know him because
he's sort of a popular Bible character. It was Samson.

· Perhaps my favorite example is Hannah. I'm not sure why I consider her
   my favorite, though. Maybe it was because I saw a lot of myself in
   her, the way I would pray earnestly for a child and even promise God
   that I would give it my all when it came to raising that child to know
   and fear the Lord. But who knows. Anyway, she was one of the two
   wives of Elkanah. The other wife had children, but Hannah did not (1
   Samuel 1:2). Each and every year they would travel to the place of
   worship. Every year Elkanah's other wife would taunt Hannah to the
   point she would be reduced to tears (1 Samuel 1:7). One time Elkanah
   even questioned why she was crying. After all, she had him. Wasn't
   he better than ten sons (1 Samuel 1:8)? When Hannah went to pray,
   she prayed with so much anguish. She finally made a vow to God. If
   He would give her a son, she would give that son back to Him (1
   Samuel 1:10-11). God ended up answering that prayer, and because
   Hannah kept her end of the bargain, which must have been extremely
   hard to do, God gave her even more children.

· Later in history we come across a woman from Shunem. Her name isn't
   even listed, and her story doesn't make up a large portion of scripture
   at all. What we do find out about her, though, is that she had no son
   and her husband was old (2 Kings 4:14). A popular prophet, Elisha,
   tells her she'll have a son, and immediately she denies it, saying he
   shouldn't get her hopes up like that (2 Kings 4:16). But sure enough, a
   year later, like Elisha said, she had her baby boy (2 Kings 4:17).

· Now into the New Testament, we come across a woman who would
   give birth to John the Baptist, Jesus' relative. Luke 1 tells us that
   Zechariah and Elizabeth were holy people. It goes on to tell us that
   they had no children because Elizabeth wasn't able to conceive (Luke
   1:7). One day when it was Zechariah's turn to burn incense in the
   temple, an angel by the name of Gabriel came to him, telling him that
   God heard his prayer, and that he and Elizabeth would have a son
   (Luke 1:13). Zechariah questioned Gabriel. He knew that he and
   Elizabeth were both old. For that, he couldn't talk until John was

born. Elizabeth, on the other hand, delighted when she became pregnant, exclaims in Luke 1:25, "How kind the Lord is! He has taken away my disgrace of having no children."

I would encourage you to read all of these women's stories in their entirety. You'll see their pain, their emotions, and how their relationships with others changed. And though I can't promise you'll have the same outcome all these seven women did, what I can promise is that God still hears your prayers and sees what you're going through.

Medical Advances

Now for those who may not believe in the Bible, there is an abundance of scientific proof that points to the reality of infertility across different cultures in different eras. For a complete history of infertility, please visit Arizona's Center for Fertility Studies' website. The link can be found in the back of the book.

- It all starts in Egypt. As early as 1900 BC, there are recorded documents discussing gynecological disorders. There was also discussion on male infertility that has been found. During this same time, medicine was permeated with magic, thus the gods played a role in childbirth. Infertile women even had their own goddess named Nephthys, and the physicians were priests to Sekhmet, the goddess of disease. And although they probably didn't have very many successful treatments for those with infertility, a lot of evidence that has been found suggests they were at least preoccupied with fertility and womanhood.

- Hippocrates, born in 460 BC, wanted to change things up. Instead of medicine being closely related to magic, he wanted it to be based more on rational thinking. Hippocrates was very well aware of infertility. He theorized causes and formulated many treatment plans.

- Little advances were made in the rest of the Greek period, as well as the Roman era. Galen (129-200 AD), however, did believe that a woman's cycle was closely related to the phases of the moon.

- During the Middle Ages, infertility was seen as a punishment. If a couple's reason for having sex wasn't for procreation, they believed their fertility would be decreased. It was also believed that infertility could be the consequence of sins committed. If a couple was going through infertility, prayer and fasting could be used to regain it. Infertility was basically seen as divine punishment, and it was a real fear during this time.

· It was the Renaissance era that really brought advances on the subject of infertility. Magic was taken completely out of the medicine equation, and the female body was becoming less mysterious. By 1562, men were recommended to put their finger in their woman's vagina after intercourse to encourage conception. As weird as this sounds, this idea is the ancestor of artificial insemination. In 1752, a man by the name of Smellie was the first to carry out experiments and describe the fertilization process. Yet, despite all these advances, infertility was seen as primarily a woman's problem. The male was rarely seen as the cause.

· The nineteenth and twentieth centuries are where medical advances really took off. In 1898, scientists figured out that fertilization was when the egg and sperm united. In 1978, the first test-tube baby was born in England, her in-vitro sister born just three years later in 1981. It was 1981 where the first IVF baby was born in the United States. Every year more and more is done to understand infertility and ways in which to treat it. Slowly, infertile women are no longer being seen as condemned members of society.

Your Family Tree

Just like infertility could be seen within the family tree during the Bible (Sarah, Rebekah, her daughter-in-law, and then Rachel, Rebekah's daughter-in-law), so, too, it is possible your own family tree includes members that have gone through infertility. This is especially true if the infertility you're dealing with is due to genetics.

At the beginning of this book I mentioned that I really had no clue anyone was going through infertility in my own family circle. It was after my miscarriage when everyone seemed to have come out in the open with their own struggle. Although my grandma never dealt with infertility, I found out she had a miscarriage. One of her daughters, my aunt, couldn't have children for a very long time. It was after they had adopted two boys from Korea that they finally had their own biological child, and a second one a while later. I found out that an aunt on my other side of the family also struggled to get pregnant and miscarried once. Also, cousins near my age from both my family as well as my husband's family came forward, sharing with me that they were having a really tough time as well so they understood what I was experiencing. Having said all of this, it became clear that there is some history with infertility in my family. Unfortunately, it's probably going to continue to live on as well.

Knowing people of various civilizations across space and time, even those within your own family line, dealt with infertility is a good thing. It's comforting and reassuring to know that the condition you're experiencing is not rare or new. There are professionals out there trying to get a deep understanding on infertility, which means there's hope. There's even a sense of fitting in, knowing that our ancestors might know a thing or two when it comes to the struggle to conceive.

16

Show Business

The second thing we all need to remember about our infertility journey is that this is not something that is happening because of who we are. Infertility can actually happen to any living soul on earth. No one is immune from it. What this means is that even those richer, more famous, or even more powerful than ourselves can and do sometimes struggle when it comes to trying to conceive.

Infertility is a disease that affects all walks of life. It could care less if you were rich or poor, skinny or fat, white or black or any other skin color, educated or uneducated, or anything else. No amount of money, fame, background, connections, or type of upbringing can keep infertility from knocking at the doors of whom it wishes to. Those things might help them afford to do treatments or whatever else they seem fit to get them through this time, but they will not keep them from knowing the pain of wanting a child and not being able to have one.

Does that seem possible to you? I know that oftentimes we look at celebrities and those in great authority as people who are far better than us. They seem to always have their life together, and bad things never seem to happen to them whatsoever. But this couldn't be further from the truth! Sometimes, perhaps even more than we know, those we hold higher than ourselves actually don't have it all like they might claim to.

The Rich and Famous

Popsugar.com is a website owned by POPSUGAR, Inc. They are a global media and technology company that informs, entertains, and inspires action based on the content they write. You can find articles on their site in a ton of different categories, including parenting, food, love, fashion, fitness, and even celebrities.

An article that was originally posted in November of 2015 and again updated in November of 2016, shared 25 celebrities that suffered with infertility. I'm not going to go through and list them all, but I do want to share the stories of some of them.

- · Mariah Carey. Almost everyone knows this famous singer. What many may not know, however, is that she had to turn to acupuncture and fertility treatments in order to get pregnant with the twins that she has. She has also suffered from one miscarriage, which put her on progesterone.

- · Gwen Stefani. She is also a popular singer, having gotten her start in a band called No Doubt. Although she was able to conceive twice before, trying for her third proved to be a hardship. The article didn't share if she did anything to help her finally conceive for the third time, but we do know that it took at least a couple of years.

- · Nicole Kidman. This famous actress, once married to Tom Cruise and now married to popular country singer, Keith Urban, has a long history of infertility. While married to Tom Cruise, the two decided to adopt when infertility got in the way of having their own children. She was in complete shock when she found out she was pregnant with her daughter after having been married two years to Keith Urban. However, infertility reared its ugly head again because when the couple tried for another, they had to go the route of surrogacy to achieve it. Altogether, Nichole Kidman has had ectopic pregnancies, miscarriages, and has undergone fertility treatments. So, she definitely knows a thing or two about how horrible infertility can be.

- · Courteney Cox. This famous actress' story I know quite well because I am a huge fan of her show, Friends. Not only did her character, Monica, on Friends deal with infertility, but her and her husband at the time did as well. She shared in the article that she has had many miscarriages and many rounds of IVF. What she came to find out was that getting pregnant was never the issue. It was staying pregnant. And it was all because of something in her blood. As soon as she would be pregnant, her body would attack the fetus. Talk about an example where your body is totally betraying you!

  Before I move on to the next celebrity, I have to share some of Courteney's journey with you that she originally shared with Matt Lauer on Dateline NBC. After just having one of her miscarriages, she had to tape an episode of <u>Friends</u> where her co-star <u>Jennifer Aniston</u>, who played Rachel, was giving birth. Can you imagine having just gone through a horrific, painful experience and then have to not only be funny (<u>Friends</u> is a comedy after all), but act out a scene where someone else is actually having a baby? Talk about difficult.

· <u>Kim Kardashian</u>. The Kardashians are always in the news it seems like, <u>Kim</u> having her fair share of things the media likes to gossip about. With regards to her infertility, however, it's not a made-up story. <u>Kim</u>, herself, has actually been pretty open about her struggle to get pregnant with baby number two. She was actually to the point where she was considering a surrogate. What she had said to <u>POPSUGAR</u> about emotions hits home to us all. She claims hysterically crying at some points and then being hopeful at others was quite the rollercoaster.

· <u>Jimmy Fallon</u>. This funny guy found a lot of reasons to be, well, not so funny. The five years of infertility that his wife and he endured were depressing and hard on everyone he claims. The couple does have two daughters now, though, thanks to using a surrogate both times.

· <u>Sarah Jessica Parker</u>. She and her famous husband, <u>Matthew Broderick</u>, also went through secondary infertility. They had a son together, and then after years and years of trying to expand their family, surrogacy was the way to go.

· <u>Brooke Shields</u>. This actress made the same common mistake we all tend to, and that is we think that when we're simply ready to have a baby, it'll happen. She obviously learned the truth, too. After having been diagnosed with cervical dysplasia, she tried IVF. After a miscarriage, she was finally able to welcome two girls.

· <u>Céline Dion</u>. <u>Céline</u> is probably one of my favorite singers of all time. Her voice is something out of this world. Her infertility experience not so much. She claims that her one miscarriage and IVF treatments were so exhausting physically and emotionally. We understand, <u>Céline</u>!

· <u>Hugh Jackman</u>. This talented actor and his wife went through a lot of infertility before they decided to adopt. He claims that adoption was always in their plan, it's just they didn't know where. After doing IVF and having miscarriages, adoption seemed like the thing to do now instead of later.

· Rod Stewart. He's another well-known singer, albeit an older one by now. He and his wife went through nearly two years of infertility before conceiving their second son on their third IVF attempt.

· Giuliana Rancic. For those who may not be aware of who she is, she is a television personality, having been on E! News a long time. She and her husband were very open about their infertility struggle. In fact, she is probably the first celebrity I heard of that was going through infertility, besides Courteney Cox that is. Giuliana has documented that she went through two IVFs. One didn't take and the other ended in a miscarriage. She was then diagnosed with breast cancer. She and her husband ended up using a surrogate for the third try in order to have their son.

· Sherri Shepherd. Sherri was once a co-host of the popular show, The View. Her story is rather interesting in that not only did she struggle quite a bit of time trying to conceive, but once she did with twins, she miscarried one of them. The one that remained was born prematurely and almost died.

If you go to POPSUGAR's website, you can read the entire article and see all 25 of the celebrities that are in there. In no way, though, is this all of them. Having done some research, I have found other sites that listed a couple of other celebrities with infertility. And, of course, there are probably many of them that haven't even shared their story, whether it be because they like to keep their personal life private as much as they can, or perhaps they feel that if people knew they were struggling with something that their image would be ruined. I don't think anyone really knows the total number of rich and famous people who have gone and are going through infertility. But that's not the point. The point is that they can struggle with it just like you and me.

Knowing that infertility can happen to anyone helps us feel like life may be more fair than we realized. In my opinion, it also pushes any thoughts of unworthiness or inferiority out the window.

17

Survey Says

The third thing to remember about our infertility journey is that everything you may experience or feel during this time is all common.

I actually conducted a very short, informal survey that well over hundred women from around the world participated in. Both women who are currently going through infertility and women who had gone through infertility are represented. At first, I created this survey because I was just curious if other women had the same thoughts and experiences as me. I thought it would also be a good way to figure out what direction I wanted to take with this book.

However, after results started pouring in, it became obvious to me that the survey needed to be a chapter all on its own. I know that the number of women that participated is such a tiny fraction of the complete infertility picture, but even that small portion spoke great volumes. What I originally thought would be pretty one-sided, was actually not. Do you know what that means? I think it means that anything and everything is possible when talking about infertility. Everything is normal, and yet there really is no real normal because it's different for each and every one of us. The results were the very definition of common.

Once you read through the survey yourself, I think you'll quickly realize that your story is pretty typical within the infertility community.

Simple Questions, Real Answers

Now like I said, don't expect anything too amazing when it comes to the types of questions I asked. This was just a very brief, straightforward survey. I could have asked hundreds of more questions at least, but stuck with just topics I knew for sure would be discussed in this book. Again, the only purpose behind any of this was to get an idea of what other women went through or are going through. For ease in reading, I'll list the question and then the results, as well as any thoughts I deem important to share.

- **Question:**   Did/Do you avoid special occasions?

Answer: 42% of the women said, "Yes."
21% of women said, "No."
37% of women said, "Occasionally."

The special occasions I was referring to here were baptisms, dedications, Mother's Day, baby showers, and the like. I definitely would have said, "Yes," and that's how I figured everyone else would have responded, too. However, I was a little surprised that it actually ended up being pretty even across the board. I guess we're not all alike, and that's a good thing!

Question: Did/Does your journey bring you closer or further from God?

Answer: 63.64% of women said, "Closer."
29.29% of women said, "Further."
7.07% of women said, "Not religious."

It was refreshing to see that a lot of women grew or are growing closer to God, yet it's totally common to not. After all, like I shared in some previous chapters, the way we view God completely changes in the midst of infertility. And, of course, for those of you who aren't religious, there won't be a change in anything because there's nothing to have a change in.

Question: How long did it take you to conceive?

Answer: 49% of women said, "Haven't yet."
25% of women said, "One to two years."
11% of women said, "Three to four years."
15% of women said, "Five plus years."

These results prove two things. The first is that I had almost the same number of women who already went through infertility as those who are currently going through it. The second thing these results prove is that once you're diagnosed with infertility, there's no real telling how long it'll take to conceive, if you do at all. There's a slightly higher percentage towards the beginning, but after that, the rate is pretty steady at a low teen's rate. I should have asked if anyone tried for ten years or more because I know there's many of those out there as well, perhaps even yourself. My guess would be, though, that the longer you try, the higher chance you'll either have conceived or have sought other methods to expanding your family.

Question: Have you ever had a miscarriage or stillbirth?

Answer: 53% of women said, "Yes."
  47% of women said, "No."

It's easy to think miscarriages and stillbirths go hand in hand with infertility. While it's absolutely possible to have infertility, and go through miscarriages or stillbirths, keep in mind that just because someone has a miscarriage or stillbirth, it doesn't mean they have infertility. They are separate. Doesn't mean the pain is any different, it just means they're not one in the same thing. The point of this question was to get a general sense of the rate of loss among those with infertility. I have to admit that these results surprised me a little. I know miscarriages, especially, happen more often than we think, but over half of these women surveyed had some kind of loss. That's higher than the professional statistics say. How tragic!

Question: How did/are you try/trying to conceive?

Answer: 38% of women said, "Medically."
  9% of women said, "Naturally."
  2% of women said, "Waiting it out."
  51% of women said, "A mix of everything."

I'm a little surprised that the number of women going the natural route isn't higher because it always seems like there's hype around going organic, using essential oils, staying away from GMOs, etc. Not that any of those things are wrong in any way. It's just I figured being natural in many areas would carry over into infertility, making it more than just a measly 9% of women who claim to go the natural route. The number of women that are doing a little bit of everything is right where I figured it would be. After all, I think most of us do whatever we can within our means to get that dream baby.

Question: How did/does infertility affect sex?

Answer: 3.03% of women said, "Sex is better."
34.34% of women said, "Sex is the same."
62.63% of women said, "Sex is worse, too routine, lost its spontaneity."

No surprise here. However, it would be nice to know what those 3.03% of women are doing that makes their sex life better! Maybe they tried or are trying one of the sex games I mentioned? Ha, ha! In all seriousness, though, I totally would have sided with the majority on this one.

Question: How did/do you react to pregnancy news?

Answer: 2% of women said, "It doesn't bother me."
44% of women said, "It depends on who."
54% of women said, "It bothers me."

I wish I could have been one of the 2%. It would be nice to be able to hear pieces of news and not be bothered by it. However, there were times I just couldn't handle it. I wouldn't say it was all the time so I guess I resonate with the 44% of women who said, "It depends on who." Especially when the "who" was either someone really close to me, or someone who I judged as shouldn't have gotten pregnant in the first place.

Question: Did/does anyone else know your struggle?

Answer: 5.1% of women said, "No one."
51.02% of women said, "Only close family and friends."
43.88% of women said, "Everyone."

For me, it was pretty obvious to some that my husband and I were struggling to get pregnant. Does anyone know all the tears I shed and emotional rollercoasters I frequented? No, not really. Well, my husband does. This is only because I'm a private person. I didn't want everyone to know everything. For others, it's almost like therapy to have people know. Either way, it's great! You've got to do what makes you comfortable and what's going to help you thrive during this time in your life.

- **Question:** What type of infertility did/do you have?

  Answer: 9.19% of women said, "Male."
  48.98% of women said, "Female."
  10.2% of women said, "Both."
  31.63% of women said, "Unexplained."

I'm not too surprised with any of this. I kind of thought male infertility would be a little higher and the unexplained infertility a little lower, but I think that these results aren't too far off from what the grander scheme of things seem to show.

- **Question:** Did/do you receive enough support?

  Answer: 36% of women said, "No. I feel alone."
  57% of women said, "Sometimes."
  17% of women said, "Yes. I receive plenty."

This question right here is the point of why I wanted to write this book. Too many women are struggling with infertility and not getting the help they need. Too many women, I say! This has got to change. I'm hoping that my book is at least a tiny weeny step forward in the right direction.

Where Do You Fit In?

Looking at this survey, how would you have responded? Would you have chosen what the majority did? Or are there times where you fit in with the select few? Whichever way you would go, you can see that at least one other person did as well!

Knowing others feel and experience what you do helps you feel less crazy, that you fit in, and it just validates everything that's going on in your world. Perhaps you're more common and normal than you thought?

The fourth thing that we need to remember is that contrary to what we may think or feel, the reality is that we're not alone! We've already briefly discussed how our ancestors also had to deal with infertility and the fact that even the rich and famous sometimes also struggle to conceive. I can totally understand, though, if those two groups of people aren't enough to get you thinking you're not alone.

But what if I shared with you some examples from "real" women? I'm talking about the everyday kind of women; women like you and me. Well, in this rather lengthy chapter, that is exactly what I will do. What you're about to read is individual stories from many women that prove you aren't the only one dealing with infertility. Many others are out there! So, if you can't resonate with the oldies or even the richies, I'm sure you'll be able to resonate with at least one of these examples.

Real Infertility Stories

The stories you are about to encounter are written out exactly as the women shared it. I didn't have any guidelines as to how it should be written or what they should include. Therefore, everything you'll read is straight from their heart. Some of them will be very short and to the point, mostly going over the logistics of their journey. Other stories are more in-depth, sharing the emotional and physical aspects of infertility. Some stories are complete, meaning the woman is no longer going through infertility. Other stories are not complete, meaning infertility is still very real to them as they still seek to get pregnant or find ways to add to their family. A few of the stories are from a while ago, but most are from right here and now in 2017. You'll see many different endings: incomplete endings, getting pregnant, adopting, and even deciding to remain a family of two. All stories are different, but all share the same theme: the difficulty of having a baby they long for. My hope is that you'll see yourself and your journey in some parts of these stories so that you feel understood, validated, inspired, and even hopeful.

To start off, I will share my complete story first. I have shared bits and pieces throughout the book, but it'll be laid out in detail here. After that, I am just going to share the stories in alphabetical order. For the sake of the women involved, I am only sharing the first name and then their story. None of these women are getting paid to share either. They all voluntarily shared their vulnerability, hoping that it'll inspire you and many others around the world.

So, without further ado, here we go!

My Story

Have you ever regretted something that you wished for? I have. In fifth grade, after watching the video about how a woman's body changes, I begged God to not let me get my period until college or later. I was so afraid that I'd have an accident and be further mocked at school. Night after night I'd plead with God to please just hold off letting my period come. I guess I figured the older I was when it came, the more I'd be able to control what all went on with it. Never in a million years did I think that God would grant me that request, and never did I once think about how this would impact my fertility.

Come high school, all my friends either had their periods or were just starting to get them. By 16, I was basically the odd woman out. My body was changing in all the right ways, but still no period. As each day and month passed, I started feeling left out and as if something was wrong with me. I took it upon myself to see a doctor so that I could get checked out. They couldn't answer as to why my periods weren't showing because all tests came back normal. Though relieved nothing was found wrong, I still wondered. I wondered why my period hadn't shown up. I wondered if it would even come. I started to even wonder what that would mean for me in the future.

Fast forward to college. I just completed my first year. I had lost some weight. It was now summer time and I'm living back at home. My lower abdomen was feeling a little odd, and when I went to the bathroom I was shocked to find some blood in my underwear. I smiled, thinking it was about time something happened! And then it hit me. I suddenly remembered what I had prayed so much for back in elementary school! God literally answered that prayer of mine! I began to feel like more of a woman. I felt grown up, like part of the club. Little did I know that my journey didn't stop there.

For three months, my period came regularly. Then, slowly and surely, they started to disappear. I'd go months without a cycle, and I knew that this couldn't be normal. However, because I wasn't even dating or thinking about having kids or any of that, I never pursued any other tests. I just accepted that this was how my body was.

When I did start getting serious with my now husband, I told him all that was going on. It didn't scare him one bit like I thought it might. He was willing to have me regardless if we could have our own children or not (and by this time I was strongly beginning to think about how this would all play out).

A couple of months before we got married I went on birth control to regulate my body, and we knew we didn't want to have kids right away. We wanted to enjoy the honeymoon phase. After being married for a month, I thought I was pregnant because my period was late. I remember being a little scared because we just weren't ready yet. We had a small apartment, we hadn't even lived together that long yet. We didn't have much time to ourselves. All selfish reasons, I know, but that was what went through my mind at that time. My period finally did show up, much to my relief (at the time). Had I known what journey we had in front of us, I would have gladly taken a pregnancy then.

The pregnancy scare actually got us thinking about having a family, though. Our original thought was to wait two years and then start trying. However, having a short time there thinking we might be pregnant made us think two years may be too long. On top of some of the issues with my body going on, we decided to just stop taking the birth control and see what God had in store. This was almost three months after getting married so about six weeks after the pregnancy scare.

Four or five months later, we both went to the doctor to just get checked out. My doctor already knew my history. We wanted to approach the idea with the doctor that we wanted to have a family so she referred us to an actual OB/GYN. The OB/GYN got me started right away on Clomid and wanted to do a HSG, as well as having a semen analysis done on my husband. My husband checked out fine. My HSG was fine. The second month on Clomid I was pregnant!

Everything was going along fine. At eight weeks pregnant, we started telling people. We were so ecstatic and couldn't hold it in! At eleven weeks, the last of those we needed to tell finally found out. We were just getting to the twelve-week mark, the second trimester. You know, the time where they say the risk of a miscarriage is significantly less.

February 23, 2007. I remember that day clearly. We were at a church event and I had to go to the bathroom. When I saw a small amount of brown blood on my underwear, my heart stopped. A part of me knew what news I would soon find out. I told my husband, and the two of us rushed to the hospital. They did an ultrasound and, sure enough, no heartbeat. In fact, they said the baby only measured at eight weeks. It just took my body that extra four weeks to figure out I wasn't pregnant anymore. I was devastated. I left the hospital okay, but as soon as I got into the truck, I bawled. My husband was right there with me, sad as well. Needless to say, we didn't go back to the church event. We went straight home. I called my mom, but my husband had the horrible job of telling everyone else that we miscarried. It wasn't easy. It sucked.

Losing my baby was hard. What made it even harder was that a close friend of mine from the church we attended was pregnant as well. In fact, she was only a couple of weeks behind me. She told me more than once that she wasn't looking to get pregnant yet and that it was a surprise. What was an exciting adventure, us being pregnant together, turned out to be an excruciating heartache. She got to keep her baby when I lost mine. My relationship with her has never been the same. Actually, now that we don't even go to the same church anymore, we don't even speak to one another.

Back to my story, my OB/GYN said that we could try again in six weeks so we did. We were put back on Clomid. This time the medicine didn't really work. A part of me was relieved. I wanted a baby, but I was so afraid that if I got pregnant again, I'd go through another miscarriage, and that is something I wouldn't wish on my worst enemy. We tried a couple more months and we still didn't end up pregnant. At this time, though, I had heard of some natural herbs that I wanted to try. With my OB/GYN's blessing, we stopped Clomid and started trying those herbs.

The first was soy isoflavones. My cousin had used it and it helped her to ovulate so I wanted to see if it would help me out as well. This herb did absolutely squat for me. So, I quickly turned to the next herb I wanted to try, which was Vitex. I did get a cycle out of Vitex, but a very long one that included some spotting. By the end of 2007 I was done with herbs. My husband and I went back to the OB/GYN to go back on Clomid.

Having done quite a few rounds of Clomid already, my doctor prescribed the highest dosage he was comfortable with. If a couple rounds of that didn't work, we already knew that next in line were to take shots. I was not comfortable with having shots, but tried to prepare my mind that they might just be in my future. The first round of Clomid was a flop. The second also. At this point I just wanted to give up. I didn't know why it wasn't working now like it had worked before. I was frustrated, depressed, and increasingly getting angry because by now almost all our friends were having babies. We were being left in the dust.

Through the midst of all the pain, God did speak to me. He was whispering to me something I did not want to do. He was telling me to give it all up and trust Him. I wanted to have a baby. Not doing anything about that meant having a baby would probably never happen. Why on earth would God tell me to do that? It got so clear to me that I was meant to stop treatments that I told my husband about it to get his opinion. He said it was up to me what I wanted to do. At the beginning of 2008, I made the tough decision to tell my OB/GYN that we weren't going to do any more Clomid, or shots, or anything. We were just going to take some time off. Again, he was supportive, which was helpful.

I thought that by listening to God I'd get pregnant. Here I was doing what God called me to do. He'd get me pregnant, right? Not right away! Two years later, to my complete surprise, I found out I was pregnant. This time, we got to keep our baby. Our first son was born November 5, 2010.

Knowing we wanted more kids, we never used protection after having our firstborn. We didn't know how long it would take so why bother messing with any of that stuff? When our son was just over the age of two, I remember feeling occasionally nauseous and was having a tough time going for walks. I would get out of breath so easily. It dawned on me that I might be pregnant. Sure enough, I was! July 12, 2013, we welcomed our second son.

I never would have guessed this is how my journey would have played out. I don't think anyone goes into trying to conceive, thinking it'll be hard. I know I didn't. And I know that I may not have done as many things as others or that my journey may not be as long as others, but it's still a journey and it has forever changed the way I view fertility. It's also made me realize that I need to be careful what I wish for because I just might get it all, and then some I don't want. (Those words remind me of a song by the talented rock star, Chris Daughtry, called "Home.")

Though my story ended happily, I hurt for those that have yet had that experience. It is now my goal to be there for others.

Amy's Story

Trust. That word means a lot to us, but I am finding that it means a great deal more than I ever could have imagined in my walk with God, a walk that includes two journeys of secondary infertility. My husband and I have been through 12 miscarriages, 13 babies in Heaven, and 3 viable pregnancies, with 4 miracle babies on Earth.

James 1:2-4 - "Consider it pure joy, my brothers, whenever you face trials of many kinds because you know that the testing of your faith develops perseverance. Perseverance must finish its work so that you may be mature and complete, not lacking anything."

Our first child was conceived easily. In fact, we weren't even trying. I ovulated a week earlier than I ever had in the last two years of tracking my cycles. Having been diagnosed with PCOS at 18 and going through two early miscarriages when I was young, lead me to wonder if I would ever have children. But I had hope. And so, in January of 2010, with grateful hearts, we welcomed a healthy son.

Four months later my husband and I would lose our first baby together at nine weeks. My body had a hard time and I ended up bleeding for two months. A month shy of two years after the birth of our eldest, we welcomed healthy, but premature, twins into the world. Their journey wasn't as easy. While it technically took three months to conceive them, we had to stop trying after two months because I was no longer ovulating or having a cycle. We focused on getting healthy, and I lost 20 pounds while my husband lost 40 pounds. When we tried again, we were shocked to discover we would be having twins. When they were three and four months old, we had back-to-back early losses. At this point, all three of the miscarriages I had with my husband were while we were on birth control. My husband came to me and said he felt God put it on his heart that He did NOT want us on birth control and that it was harming me. So, we stopped preventing.

Four months later we would miscarry again. And then we wouldn't conceive on our own again for another 16 months. In that time, we ended up turning to fertility drugs, which resulted in two more miscarriages and a third cycle that completely failed. I did a major diet change, hoping for the success we saw before the twins. I used fertility supplements to force ovulation. This time we made it far enough to see our baby alive before the baby died.

Psalm 34:17-19 - "The righteous cry out, and the Lord hears them; he delivers them from all their troubles. The Lord is close to the brokenhearted and saves those who are crushed in spirit. A righteous man may have many troubles, but the Lord delivers him from them all."

I cried out to God that April and said, "I can't do this anymore, God. You need to clearly tell me what to do because I'm losing hope. I keep feeling like I have a son out there that needs to be born but I keep miscarrying. Just tell me, Lord, what You want!"

My doctor told me there was nothing more he could do for me and I got referred to an RE for September. In July, however, God answered my prayers. After a dream where I had a baby, I awoke to the voice of God telling me, "You can trust in Me or you can keep trying to force it. If you trust in Me, I will give you a child."

So, we let it go, canceling with the RE. We kept tracking my cycle so I could get on the right medications (just-in-case medications, as we had no answers to our losses), but we stopped all supplements and drugs. In September, I ovulated for the first time on my own in 16 months.

My doctor immediately called my RE to get me in. They said they wanted two blood draws, confirming pregnancy first. My blood draws showed rising pregnancy hormones, but dangerously low progesterone levels. Levels so low that I would definitely get a period even while pregnant because they weren't enough to keep it away. I prayed to God to have the RE get me in that day. My doctor came into the room and said if you can drive over fast they can see you right now. The RE told me there had been an error that had never happened before. Her schedule is normally so packed, it takes weeks to months to get in.

That was where the good news ended. She spent the next hour explaining to me how I would always miscarry. My low progesterone meant something was wrong with the baby and those babies weren't worth saving. She told me she was 99% sure I would come in the next week with my blood levels showing not pregnant. I was devastated and broke down so she grudgingly gave me the medication to help my progesterone level.

Matthew 19:26 - "But Jesus looked at them and said to them, "With men this is impossible, but with God all things are possible.""

I went in a week later to a very high HCG level. I was still pregnant, and it was going well. God showed me beyond a shadow of a doubt that greater is He who is in us, than he who is in the world. That following May I welcomed a completely healthy son into the world.

Psalm 37:3-6 - "Trust in the Lord and do good; dwell in the land and enjoy safe pasture. Delight yourself in the Lord and he will give you the desires of your heart. Commit your way to the Lord; trust in him and He will do this; He will make your righteousness shine like the dawn, the justice of your cause like the noonday sun."

Because of all we had been through and where my husband had felt God leading us, we decided to completely trust our fertility to God. To never prevent His blessings again. We also learned my condition made birth control very risky for my health with 3x greater the risk of stroke and blood clots, and women already face a high risk on hormonal birth control. God had been protecting me even before we truly were seeking Him and welcoming Him into our lives.

I wish I could say things got better, but as I said, this is a story of two journeys of secondary infertility. Since my youngest was born, we've lost five more babies. Two made it to ten weeks, our last one we saw alive twice before she died. We've had all the testing and are still without answers.

I'm learning to trust God that there is no healing in the answers, only in Him. To see all the ways in which He works our hurts and our heartbreaks into good. How He makes us new, refines us. How he loves us.

And I'm learning that there is still hope. For all of us.

Psalm 39:7 - "And now, Lord, what do I wait for? My hope is in You."

Another Amy's Story

Yesterday, my doctor placed a fertilized egg in my uterus. After spending many years of my life trying to avoid pregnancy, and the past nearly three years trying for the opposite, this is the closest I've ever been to being pregnant. There have been plenty of times I thought I was pregnant, but this is the first time I have concrete evidence that it's actually probable. Plus, the doctors having assured me there was a 90% success rate with this procedure.

The past few years have been such a rollercoaster, and while I'm doing my best to stay positive, I still have moments of doubt that it's really possible, that it's really, finally, happening. I've found no better training ground for living with uncertainty, though that doesn't necessarily mean it's gotten any easier.

The crazy thing is I'm not one of those people who grew up dreaming of having kids someday, and I spent the majority of my childbearing years actively determined not to have kids or just figuring it was something I could worry about some day in the future. Maybe that makes all of this a little easier for me than for a woman who has had motherhood as a lifetime goal, but I think that once you decide you do want something, it doesn't really matter how long you've had that desire.

When I met the man I would marry, a man who was very clear about his desire for kids, it was time for me to figure out where I really stood on the issue, and after much soul searching, I decided that, yes, this was something I wanted. Throughout that process, I remember thinking how unfair it was that I could spend all this time deciding if I wanted something, and only once I decided and tried to get it might I discover I couldn't have it.

I had no idea what lay ahead, of course, and I really didn't think we would have any problems getting pregnant. We got married about two years after we first met, when I was 36, and I remember thinking I wanted to have some more time as a couple before we started trying so we decided to wait a few years. It never occurred to me to build in time for it to take a while, or how much the clock was ticking during those years.

I'm now 41, and assuming this pregnancy takes, I'll be 42 1/2 when our baby is born. I never thought I'd become a mother at this age, but it is what it is. I never thought age really mattered until it did, and it was the only explanation the doctors had for why I've had so much trouble getting pregnant.

We had agreed that we'd keep things natural, trying things like supplements and acupuncture to help increase the odds, but not going as far as outright fertility treatments. We weren't interested in committing to the cost, the complicated procedures, the manipulation of my cycle until the natural way wasn't working and we were running out of options.

While living abroad, we learned about a fertility clinic that came highly recommended, and where the costs were much lower than the numbers I'd always heard flung around in the U.S. We decided to give it a shot. After one failed attempt, here we are, a five-day-old embryo floating in my womb and all our hopes pinned on it.

One of the reasons I wanted to share my story is because I think this is a topic that not enough people talk about, and I'd like to see it more out in the open. Yet as my efforts to get pregnant have gotten ever more complicated, I understand why people don't talk about it, particularly while they're in the middle of it. The more people who know we're trying, the more people I feel I need to keep updated on how things are going, especially at this point when every step is scheduled and programmed. And when things don't go well, I don't necessarily want to talk about it with lots of people. But I have been grateful for those who did know, and were available to support us through the tough times.

Most of the people in my life whom I have shared this experience with and who have actively supported me along the way have never struggled with infertility. While they've been supportive, it's not quite the same as connecting with people who have been through something similar and can share their experience and wisdom. But if no one talks about having been through this, we don't know whom to turn to, who can understand and be a source of support. I guess this is why I've told quite a few people over the years that we were trying, hoping that at some point I would find someone on the same path (or who'd been there in the past). I haven't found many, which may be why many women turn to the Internet for solace and community. But the little I read on message boards and online forums led me to decide that I didn't want to get my hopes up or be disappointed based on anyone else's experience; I wanted to have my own experience.

I hope the stories in this book help other women know that they're not alone, yet I hope they don't get disappointed or disillusioned comparing their situations to the ones shared here. Each woman's experience is individual, each of us is on our own journey. It can be a very long, lonely road, but I try to remember what I heard in a meditation recently: "Everything is unfolding perfectly." It can be hard to believe that sometimes, but it's all I have.

Angela's Story

My infertility story starts in September of 2013. My husband and I were nervous and excited when we decided we were ready to start growing our family. Unfortunately, I was under the illusion that these things happen quickly as it had been my experience with other people around me. You can imagine my disappointment when I read my first negative pregnancy test. Little did I know how many more would follow.

Infertility brought a wide range of emotions. Loneliness. Jealousy. Anger. Disappointment. Despair. Grief. Yet, with these difficult emotions also came a tremendous amount of growth. Until this point in my life, I hadn't experienced such a difficult season so I had a lot to learn about navigating and responding to adversity.

The first year of trying was the hardest since we didn't tell anyone that we were trying to get pregnant. Every month I bore the disappointment on my shoulders with no one to help lighten the load. Month after month, as the desire to get pregnant grew and grew, an emptiness started to grow in my heart. I felt so alone, and it seemed that everyone else in the world became pregnant whenever they wanted. During that time, my sister-in-law and one of my best friends got pregnant. I struggled with trying to be happy for them while at the same time trying to deal with my grief. It felt as though people were moving on without me, going on to the stage of parenthood, and leaving me behind.

As more time went by, I began to doubt if I would ever be able to have a child of my own. That reality crushed my spirit. I couldn't bear the thought of never knowing the joy of giving life. I knew that adoption was an option, but I wanted nothing to do with it. I was angry that there were unwanted children out there when I wanted nothing more than to carry and give birth to a child of my own.

My faith suffered but eventually grew under the pain and struggle with infertility. I was angry at God at first and questioned His love for me. It came to the point where I had to decide if I was going to trust a God who would allow me to go through this pain. As I learned more about the character of God, I realized that He was using this suffering to draw me closer to Him. His purpose wasn't to watch me suffer, but to teach me to lean on Him through the suffering. Despite this realization, it didn't make the journey easy. I went through a lot of growing pains as God taught me about my lack of control over my life and surrendering to His will and plan.

After about a year of trying, we saw a fertility specialist and officially received the diagnosis of infertility. As difficult as it was to hear, it validated our struggle and we began sharing our journey with more people. As I shared, I discovered that there were so many women who had walked this journey before me or were currently going through it. Hearing other women share their stories lightened the burden of my disappointment and sadness. I found great comfort and hope from being able to share my feelings with those who understood what I was going through.

Despite the support, infertility was a roller coaster. Every month had its cycle of emotions: hope, expectancy, waiting, disappointment, despair, and then it would start all over again. It was exhausting. My faith was on a wild coaster as well. Some days I was optimistic, trusting that God had the best in mind for me. Other days I was tired and empty, not sure I could handle one more negative pregnancy test, and again questioning what God was doing and why my prayers weren't being answered.

In June 2015, after 21 months of disappointment and three failed IUIs, my husband and I decided to take a break from fertility treatments and trying to get pregnant. I was burnt out, didn't have any fight left in me, and just needed the summer to clear my mind from ovulation tests, fertility drugs, and pregnancy tests.

The next month, my period was a little late, but I knew it would show its ugly face soon enough. At least this time I was ready and prepared for it. As each day passed, I would get my hopes up, but quickly suppress them as I knew better than to set myself up for disappointment. The doctors had only given us a 5% chance of getting pregnant on our own so I wasn't going to waste a pregnancy test on this month.

After a few more days, I couldn't stop wondering anymore; I had to know one way or another. I took a pregnancy test, but unlike other months, I couldn't bear to watch it. But out of the corner of my eye, I thought I saw two blue lines. I got my husband out of bed, we looked at the test together and saw two lines, clear as day. It was one of the most surreal moments of my life. After seeing so many negative tests, I could barely believe my eyes. Through our tears, we immediately prayed and thanked God for finally answering our prayers.

On March 15, 2016, our son was born. He is one of the happiest babies I know and he has a smile that lights up his whole face. Seeing his joy and smiles every day reminds me of God's faithfulness. I can see now that God wasn't saying, "No," to my prayers, but, "Wait." Waiting for a child was the most difficult thing I've endured, but I am grateful for it. I understand now that there was a purpose for the pain. God used it to draw me closer to Him. He exposed my fragile faith and grew it in ways that wouldn't have otherwise been possible. Infertility helped me better relate to people who are hurting, and taught me about the importance of community. The pain of infertility is deep, but the joy I have with my son is so much sweeter because of it.

Bekki's Story

When my husband and I got married, I was on birth control because we wanted to be settled before we began trying for kids. I was diagnosed with polycystic ovarian syndrome when I was in my 20s and was told getting pregnant could be difficult. We were married in May of 2014. In February of 2015 I thought I was possibly pregnant. I was feeling nauseous and had a couple other possible indicators. Both my husband and I were very excited at the thought of me being pregnant. Just when I was thinking it was time to buy a pregnancy test, I got my period. We were both so disappointed. After that, we talked about me stopping my birth control, and we agreed it was time.

So, I guess we started trying for a baby in March of 2015. In November of 2015 I had to have surgery to remove a cyst from one of my ovaries. At my follow-up appointment with my OB/GYN we discussed that we had been trying for several months to get pregnant and she said she could start me on fertility meds when I was ready. I wasn't quite ready for fertility meds yet. My husband and I agreed to try natural supplements, and I am still trying different supplements and eating healthy and praying to become pregnant. It's been two years since that first thought of possibly being pregnant.

I will probably be making an appointment with my OB/GYN to try some fertility meds in the next couple of months. My husband and I have also talked about the possibility of adoption. We want to be parents; doesn't matter how a baby comes to us. These are the facts of our journey.

The emotional side of it is more difficult to think about. I have struggled with feeling inadequate as a woman. I feel as though I've let my husband down. I have even struggled with feeling as though God doesn't think I should be a mother. It's a lot of raw emotion, and a hard thing to keep inside sometimes. But I am blessed to have a husband who won't let me struggle alone and I know that this is part of God's plan for me.

Brandy's Story

Growing up, before I had any knowledge of reproductive anatomy or biology, I dreamt, like many young girls, of having children one day, but felt like I might have troubles. I even asked my mother once what I could do if I was unable to have children. Knowing I was too young, she deflected my question and told me not to think about such things. At the onset of puberty, my cycles were irregular and uncomfortable, but all information available to me at that time stated that it was normal and could take a couple of years for a girl's cycle to regulate. I had very painful cramps and bloating, and often felt sick just before and during my period.

While my cycles did become somewhat more predictable, they were never regular and my symptoms only became worse. At the age of 18, I finally saw a doctor, who based on my complaints, prescribed birth control pills to "help regulate". During my 3 1/2 years of taking birth control pills, my cycles were regular, and I experienced decreased symptoms of PMS. However, I gained 60 pounds, dealt with recurring headaches, and struggled to deal with the stresses of college and marriage.

I stopped taking the birth control pills. My symptoms all returned with a vengeance. I experienced even more irregular cycles, discomfort, mood swings, developed cystic acne, and continued to gain weight. I saw a new doctor who, after a full lab workup, diagnosed me with polycystic ovarian syndrome. In the midst of a strenuous, accelerated course of study and earning a degree, moving a few times, and job searching, I put my health on the back burner. My husband and I moved to a new state and I stayed home for a few months to get settled in.

During those few months, I realized how bad my health had gotten. I was constantly exhausted. My hair was thinning. I had constant brain fog, body pains, and headaches. I even developed blurred vision. Not to mention I went months between cycles, and despite not being on birth control, failed to become pregnant. I finally realized I needed to see a reproductive endocrinologist, who basically told me I was too fat, and to take metformin to control my blood sugar levels, which I did not even know were an issue for me at that point. I left feeling so deflated and afraid. I tried taking the metformin, but the gastrointestinal side effects caused me to discontinue taking it. I also did not return to see the RE because insurance did not cover infertility treatments (even though I was more concerned with my health than with my fertility at that point), and because of the doctor's lack of tact and concern.

I finally found a new doctor, who was attentive and more tactful. He explained things to me in a more caring way. He encouraged me to take metformin again and to push through the discomforts, as it would subside. He also prescribed Clomid to promote ovulation. I began tracking my cycles and basal body temperature to detect ovulation. I took 10 rounds of Clomid, which is more than what is recommended. I conceived twice on Clomid, but miscarried at around four weeks on it both times.

My doctor then referred me to an infertility specialist. I decided not to go to the infertility specialist, but instead to focus on lifestyle changes. I made some radical changes to my diet and became more active. In addition, my husband and I began the process to become licensed foster parents. A few months after I made these changes, I became pregnant, naturally. Bloodwork indicated that I had low levels of progesterone so my doctor prescribed a compounded progesterone. The pregnancy was troubled, and I thought I was miscarrying several times. We received our first foster placement when I was 12 weeks pregnant. I was so overwhelmed with joy and anticipation with the little one growing inside and I was doing my best to care for and love the two little ones who had been placed in my home. I was very busy and active and distracted, but loving how my life was going at that point.

When I was 18 weeks pregnant, days away from finding out the gender of our baby, my water broke, and within a few hours, our son was born prematurely. We were heartbroken, but had an amazing support system. Thankfully, my body healed fairly quickly, and lab work revealed that I may have had a sub-chorionic hemorrhage. A few months later, I quit my job and decided to stay home to care for the foster children that were placed in our home, and to focus on my health. I continued to eat a clean diet and remained pretty active.

Less than a year later, I became pregnant again, naturally. In some research I had done, I had discovered that my pregnancy loss had lined up with incompetent cervix so I asked my doctor about it. While I couldn't be diagnosed with it after the loss we had experienced, my doctor felt like it would be wise for me to have a procedure called a cerclage (cervical stitch) as a precaution. I was prescribed progesterone again, which I took until week 18, and had an easy pregnancy. My cerclage was removed at 38 weeks. My water broke three days later, and after a Pitocin induced labor of 12 hours, I delivered my son via emergency C-section.

My son is now five years old. We adopted our two foster children two weeks after he was born. I have been unsuccessful in my attempts to regain my health again, though I have tried several times. I feel like time is slipping away and it breaks my heart when I think of the children that could have been had my health not been so hard to get under control. I have felt so many times less than a woman because my body just doesn't work the way it was designed to. But I have not given up hope. I lose motivation from time to time because it seems so daunting, but there is always hope that I will be able to maintain a healthy lifestyle so that my body will become fertile again. I have resigned that I will have to have the cerclage procedure with any and all subsequent pregnancies, but I'll do what I have to bring a baby safely into the world.

Casey's Story

I met Mr. Right the week before I started college. It took him a full year to decide that I was Mrs. Right, and then the year after that we were married. Life was heavenly, until that is, when we started talking about heaven, literally. As we commenced our life together, my husband began to see deficiencies in my spiritual life. Something was missing. I could answer all the questions correctly and serve in the nursery happily, but my heart was cold. After many months of discussions, and the Lord opening my eyes to my own self-deception, I realized that I was not saved. At 21-years-old I finally called on Jesus just as I am, a sinner, with nothing to offer Him. I asked Him to forgive me and begin the work of sanctification in my life. My heart began to understand so much of what my ears had heard for years. What a gracious God to send His Son to die for me!! Hallelujah!

Over the next few years I could see the Holy Spirit's work in my heart to grow me in Christ-likeness, but my own effort toward that goal was still wimpy. I struggled to read my Bible on a consistent basis or actually do the lesson for the Bible study I attended. I did not take personal responsibility for my own spiritual growth. I just wanted it to happen to me. In a sense, that is exactly what God allowed next. Infertility happened to me. I did not pick it – who would ever pick it?!? God was more interested in my holiness than my happiness. A baby may have made me happy for a time during those early years of marriage, but God knew that infertility would make me holier.

Years five through eight of our marriage were hard. I was a stressed, panicky wreck. My husband did not know what to do with me, and even his patience found its limits with my incessant worrying. God was asking me to trust Him and wait on Him, but I was ignoring that request. I still went to church, of course. I still tried to read my Bible regularly, but I was angry about not getting my way. When I spoke to God, I prayed for everyone else, but not myself. I didn't want to talk to God about the baby He was withholding from me.

Somewhere in that journey, I realized that the other ladies in my Bible study, the ones who had kids, were becoming godlier than me. It was as if they had found a different road, a fast track, to holiness and I could not get on the entrance ramp. Even though I was not speaking to God about my malfunctioning body, I was speaking to Him about my spiritual walk. I started to ask God for more sanctification, the kind that my friends were experiencing, even if I never had children.

There, I said it! "Lord, help me if I never have kids." I may never have kids. Is God still loving if I never have a baby? Is God still trustworthy? Do I believe He's the Great Physician that could make my body work the way so many other women's bodies do? "Lord, I want to believe. Help my unbelief."

The last few months of our infertility journey were stressful for a new reason – my grandma was dying of cancer. She needed someone to accompany her on a trip to California to visit her sister, and without the responsibilities of motherhood, I was available. She needed her only granddaughter to come sit with her one evening each week, and again, I was available. Those hours and days spent with my grandmother were invaluable. I was so thankful that God gave me the privilege of serving her that way. Thankful for my childlessness? Thankful? Yes, Lord.

That was the end of infertility for me. The last time my grandma hugged me I was pregnant with my son and I didn't know it yet. A few weeks after her funeral, my husband and I sat in a restaurant for our eighth wedding anniversary and he asked if I was pregnant. I had lost track of the month. A test the next morning confirmed it. God was granting us a son. What a delightful balm to our aching hearts!

Since then the Lord has given us the grace to praise Him at the stillborn birth of our first daughter and the joy of welcoming a second, live daughter. Through all of this, I learned that God has, "Given me relief when I was in distress. You have put more joy in my heart than they have when their grain and wine [and children] abound" (Psalm 4).

Emily's Story

We got married a little older; I was 32 and he was 34. Right after we got married my cycle started changing and I started having painful cysts. So here we are just married, both working full time, and I was finishing my bachelor degree full time. This started in June, and the beginning of December my OB told me to start seriously thinking about having a family if we were going to have one. I remember going home and just crying to my husband. We had only been married six months and now I had to tell my husband that we needed to start trying. And he stood beside me 100% from the beginning.

About six months passed and I had to switch OBs, who sent us to the infertility center where we found out that I was early premenopausal and he has a low count, but there is no good medical explanation as to why. We agreed at the start of the infertility center that we would only do IUI and not pursue anything further because we didn't want crazy amounts of debt. We did four rounds. Each month we felt that the infertility center gave us a little more information than the month before, and at the end of our journey there, they basically said they felt my husband was the problem, but never had mentioned that before, which was very frustrating.

The fertility drugs were hell. Every month the side effects were different and my amazing husband was so good about it. With each cycle, there was also the shot that made me ovulate, and he would give it to me as gently as possible. I also want to mention the dreaded HSG test. I'm so thankful that a friend of mine warned me about it beforehand! After that we took a break. Going through infertility treatments can seriously kill the romance, not to mention the cost, and nothing is covered by insurance. Since then we've also done a six-month program with a natural path and also worked with a kinesiologist.

Recently my cycles started getting worse again, and in December around our four-year anniversary, I was scheduled for an ablation procedure. I was literally gowned up and ready to go when my OB came in asking me what my symptoms were. The surgery ended up changing and I was diagnosed with endometriosis. So now when I thought our infertility journey was ending, we are still in it. I want to have the childlike faith that through Him anything is possible. Clearly our journey is not over, but there's also still the medical diagnosis nagging at the back of my mind.

Another Emily's Story

We had been together for three years and ended up breaking up for two months. The month after we got back together, I found out I was pregnant. When our daughter was born, we found out it wasn't his, but we got married anyway.

We went to the doctor because we figured three years was quite a while of being unprotected, and him being 30 and having no kids was strange. At that point, the doctor did some testing and found out that not only was his sperm count extremely low, but also his motility was slightly under what they prefer it to be, and they told us then that without IVF there was no chance of him having a baby.

That was two years ago, and a lot has changed since then. We spoke with some fertility clinics in July of 2016 and the plan was to start the IVF process in March of 2017. Then it was September 2016 and my period didn't show up. A pregnancy test confirmed we were pregnant and we didn't believe it so we bought another test. Same thing! A week later we went to the OB/GYN and they confirmed we were six weeks pregnant, due May of 2017. Even the doctor who had performed my husband's past testing was surprised, but there is no doubt that it's his and we couldn't be happier!!

Erin's Story

*Erin actually has a blog called Living Life with Character. She has given me permission to use the information from her blog, which you can find the link to at the back of this book. Though it isn't current, please do check it out as there is more information there than just on infertility.

Growing up, the word on the street (in a small town, ha ha) was, "Don't have sex before marriage because you could get pregnant". In a public school, they taught ways to protect, abstinence, and choices. I made my choice to wait. Seriously, I was scared silly about getting pregnant (even though I chose to wait anyway), and thought it would happen really quickly after we started trying to conceive.

Weeks went by.

Months went by.

Finally, years went by.

Why is this happening to us? We LOVE kids. We would make great parents. We are responsible, nurturing, caring, and loving people who would like to be blessed with kids. I truly believed that we would be parents someday; it just took a REALLY long time.

We knew we wanted kids right away. However, with people telling us we need a "year" to experience all the joys of being married, we decided to listen. About six months into marriage, we felt the desire to follow our dream of becoming parents.

Fast forward a year. No positive pregnancy tests. No joyous "OH MY GOSH!!" moments. No "CONGRATULATIONS" for us. All that was left was depression, anger, sadness, and a desire for something we could not have. It was depressing. It was lonely. It was just plain awfully emotional.

At this point, my husband told me it was time to go to the doctor (we had hit the one-year mark of actively trying so something was wrong with us). With his encouragement, I set up an appointment with our family doctor (I didn't even know where to start). When the appointment came around, my husband had recently been laid off due to the lovely economy. He said to go anyway. We had an HSA account set up with some money in it for this. As I got into the room, the doctor looked at my health chart and asked, "Oh, what does 'self-pay' mean?". My response was that my husband had recently been laid off so we are paying with it in cash. At that point, her demeanor changed as she sat down to talk to me.

She talked for the next 50 minutes. Boy, did she talk. No tests, no prescriptions, no referrals, no nothing, but a $80 charge for the appointment. She told me everything I had already found out via the worldwide web. She said that I may need to lose weight. She suggested not to pressure my husband into something since it's hard enough losing a job. She said that I was young and that I had time. She told me that I need to relax, and it will happen. She had the audacity to say, "Maybe it's not God's time for you yet; just keep trying". Now I'm a Christian and I believe in God. I fully agree that He has a plan for my life, and that it is in His timing. I also know I have choices. I have the choice to seek help from doctors. I expect doctors to help me. She did not. In fact, when I asked her should I start taking prenatal vitamins (hinting that I'd like that prescription), she said, "No." The doctor walked me out of the room to the pay counter and asked the ladies to print out all the prices for any and all tests we might need to take.

I was in tears by the end. Walking out of the doctor's office crying, paying a $80 fee, with a list of prices for tests I might need to get done; it was discouraging. I was upset. I was hurt. I was really flipping mad at that doctor. I never went back. It took me another year just to get up the guts to call another doctor to get the ball rolling. A whole, entire year.

In the fall of 2010, we went to an informational meeting at a fertility place about 30 minutes away. I had some anxiety, but they were friendly, helpful, and non-judgmental. In this informational meeting, we got a coupon for our first consultation, which went fabulous. By the next month, we had all of our tests done. We now knew what we were up against.

We had our first IUI done December 2010, which turned out to be unsuccessful. It was a sad few days. My amazing husband was right by my side, though, and we looked at the reasons why it was a good thing it didn't work out this time. (Trying to look at our glass half full!)

Then in August/September 2011 we were changed forever. There we were. Tempted in a store to go look for something that we never thought we would. At least, that's how it felt. Sneaking around, we found the right area and started to shop. There they were. Two adorable outfits. How could we decide which one to buy? It was so early. I looked at Josh and said, "Let's buy both." We were SO super excited, and as we went to pay, we kept turning corners seeing people we knew. So, the opposite way we'd go (who knew this store would be so busy on a Sunday after church?) We were giggly. We were the lovey-dovey people that couldn't keep our hands off of each other. We were the happy couple who were dodging corners and sneaking around the store. We finally made it to a register knowing our huge secret was safe. Every night since, we had the two outfits hanging in our closet. And every night we were reminded by the new hanging wardrobe and our secret.

We went to bed happy. Excited. Content. Ready.

Then, I met our doctor. Oh, how great he was. To my surprise, delivering was his favorite thing as a doctor. Without hesitation, he agreed to get an early ultrasound done that I requested. I was so relieved. Nothing felt real at this point, except for the strange aversions toward chocolate (didn't see that one coming!), constantly tired, and losing a few pounds.

The first ultrasound brought worried thoughts, but nothing 'real'. They said it was too early. We saw something on the screen, but not much. They said it just was really early, and we'll have another one.

We were very excited to see the second ultrasound, a little peanut, a heartbeat-proof. We were expecting to tell family and friends with the picture of our secret, our secret that we shopped for when we found out early on. A different lady was our ultrasound tech. An older, non-talker. As she started the ultrasound, we were not seeing anything baby-like on the screen (just a gestational sac). Nothing that I knew we should be seeing at 10 weeks. No heartbeat. No little bean shape. Tears started flowing. The ultrasound tech lady wouldn't tell us anything. Just that, "We don't know anything yet". Trying not to cry while walking out of the hospital was impossible. I couldn't keep them back. Something was wrong. I was supposed to work the next day. I walked through the door and just starting bawling. Thankfully, I was blessed with an amazing group of coworkers. Emotionally, I just couldn't work.

My amazing doctor called us, wanting us to come in. He cleared time in his day. He was flexible. I could tell he really cared for us and what we were experiencing. Trying to hold back the tears in the doctor's office, my hubby and I were trying to crack some jokes. It'd work, then I'd remember why we were there. If you knew me personally, I'm just flat out emotional. No lies! Composing myself can be hard, especially with something like this. Teary-eyed, we finally went into the exam room.

Five minutes passed. In came the nurse and immediately I asked, "Somethings wrong, isn't it?" Gently, she took a minute to pray for me, for us, for our family. The doctor finally came in, and without hesitation, I asked him. My worst fears were confirmed. He said it happens randomly and to anyone. He described to us what happened, which I already knew what it was called, a blighted ovum. (He was surprised I knew. I told him I was the research queen at my house with the help of google!) He said I would miscarry within the next few weeks. I cried. My hubby held my hand and wept, too. The doctor held our hands and prayed with us.

I was upset. Angry. God, why did you let this happen to us? We've waited for three years, and now we're the lucky ones to go through this, too? I mean, come on!

In hindsight, I guess I have won something. It's called experience. I have gained and learned some things. I've learned that God has been with us, and He certainly is our Provider. He's surrounded us with loving family, friends, and even strangers who have blessed us, prayed for us, and encouraged us. He's provided strength, direction, and a renewed passion for living life. He's shown us that we are brave, and that with Him we can go through tough things! The more we talk and are open about miscarriage and infertility, the more God shows up, the more we feel at peace with where we are at. We've learned to look at our life, to be thankful for what we have, to complain less, and to enjoy every minute of the great and not-so-great situations. We've learned that life truly does go on, and in the end, there will be a reason, a purpose for this trial, this suffering, and this sadness. And someday, I will meet this little angel who has forever changed our lives and our outlook on life. Life is precious, it is a gift, and a miracle. We miss what could have been, but are blessed with what is and what is to come.

Anyway, back to the story. Anger. Sadness. Left out. Depression. Acceptance. And finally, hope.

In all, my husband and I struggled with infertility for about 4 1/2 years. I wish I could say that I grew closer to Christ or that my faith grew during that season, but I have to admit it was completely opposite. Instead, I cried daily, felt withdrawn, and experienced bitterness due to wanting a child so badly. When I look back, I am ashamed of the person that I once was as it was not my normal me. I began to become very anxious when it came to groups of women because the first thing women tend to ask is, "Do you have kids?" or if it's a group of my friends, I'm suddenly in a kid conversation. Women seeking advice about their own kids or complaining about their kids, and I had nothing to offer. For hours. I wanted to escape. I felt like I was the odd one out.

Going through infertility was one of the most heartbreaking things I've ever gone through. It required me to be brutally honest with my husband about how I was feeling, being vulnerable with him as I cried in his arms for days. No one understood what I was emotionally going through.

Every pregnancy announcement would cause my heart to wonder when I would have a child. I avoided baby showers because I was afraid I would lose it. Eventually my sadness, anger, and feeling alone turned into bitterness. Unkind things came out of my mouth while bitter thoughts consumed my mind. How could she be a mom? She doesn't deserve kids. Wow, why is that 16-year-old keeping her baby? Doesn't she know the reality of what's coming?

My life changed when I met a woman who shared her infertility journey with me. Her story was incredible. At the time, she had one young child at home and was in the midst of another round of IVF. On top of that, the embryos were not always viable due to a rare genetic condition. Her story, her attitude, and her openness allowed me to realize that there were others struggling with infertility. It felt refreshing to talk with someone who understood the many emotions I was feeling. I realized that talking about my infertility struggles was one of the best forms of therapy for my emotional well-being.

I started talking about it more. When people would ask about kids, I would be honest with them, saying, "We're in the midst of infertility, but we would love to have kids someday." I started writing. I started posting articles on Facebook. When I started to open up and accepting that I was struggling with infertility, more people started coming to me who were also struggling with it.

The heartache of infertility, the journey of hopelessness in having a child, prepared me for what was yet to come. After the blighted ovum/miscarriage, we eventually got pregnant again (with the help of supplements). After going to the doctor for my glucose check, I asked about getting another ultrasound due to some signs. Secretly, even though I was 26 weeks along, I just wanted to see my baby again because I still was in disbelief that I was pregnant. We were scheduled for an ultrasound that day, and to much of our surprise, after the appointment, they wheeled me up to the birthing floor without telling my husband and I what was going on. After being hooked up to monitors, the nurse finally gave us the news. We were having this baby today due to being fully dilated because of an incompetent cervix. We were scared, but so happy to finally meet our guy.

After he was born, all two pounds of him, the thought of losing him never occurred to us. He was here. He was being taken care of. Days were filled at the hospital visiting him, and we always had a smile on our face because we knew that his life is such a miracle. We learned to fight for that child. We learned to stand up for his health needs, to ask questions. It was the hardship of our infertility journey that made us cherish our little boy's life and to have hope. After 78 days, our miracle came home.

Heather's Story

My husband and I have been married for almost four years. Right before we got engaged, I was diagnosed with a pituitary tumor that was secreting extra prolactin, causing amenorrhea and galactorrhea. My doctor told me, right after giving me the diagnosis, that I had a major increased risk of infertility. I had an open and honest conversation with my now husband, then boyfriend, and gave him an out. I told him that if biological kids were important to him, that I likely was not meant to be his forever partner. I knew I was called to motherhood, I just didn't know how it would present.

Well, fast forward three months later, and not only did he stick around, he proposed! We had some difficult conversations from my diagnosis date through present day regarding children. When we got married, we did not want to try for children right away because I was entering graduate school. We knew it could be difficult, but we trusted that God would prevail when we were ready (selfish thinking). Well, it came time for us to begin trying. I was faced with amenorrhea again, so more testing demonstrated my hormones were all messed up and I now had PCOS on top of my tumor. I was devastated. We continued to try, and eventually my doctor put me on Clomid. My body refused to ovulate despite my increasing dose.

I decided to send my husband for testing, during this time of trying to determine how to get my body to respond, just to make sure I was the sole issue. Unfortunately, we didn't get the news we wanted. My husband's sperm had 97% head defects, and we were told we would never conceive naturally. My doctor no longer felt like she could be of service to us and referred us to a RE.

Our process with the RE provided a ton of information, but I just became an emotional wreck. We felt more and more defeated with each passing month. We kept trying IUI after IUI with the same negative result. However, throughout this journey, I felt God talking to me more and more. He would send a message that I needed to hear on the days I needed it the most. In July, we had our sixth IUI scheduled. My husband's sperm was the worst it had ever been. My body responded poorly to this round of medication. We really felt like this IUI was just a waste of time. But then on Facebook, I came across a passage about why should we doubt the power of God related to male infertility when God performed a miracle of the fish and the loaves. I knew God meant that message for me! And more messages continued to come my way during this TWW. God kept telling me that he would provide.

Well, God did just that! I am now 34 1/2 weeks pregnant with a baby boy. I still suffer with extreme anxiety, worried that something will still go wrong, but I try to remain faithful. God is so good! His plan is always perfect. I really had to come to terms that biological children may not be in our future, but I felt God's peace with that! A favorite line from a church song is, "Give to us today what you have planned for us no matter what it is". This takes pure faith. I struggle with accepting this, but I know that God has a plan and purpose in all of our lives.

Holly's Story

My husband and I met our first year at college. We got engaged after we graduated and got married the next year. After getting married, we focused on each other and our careers for a while. We always wanted a family, we just weren't in a hurry. We had no reason to expect we would have difficulty. No one in either of our families had. Or at least they didn't talk about it. I had regular cycles. My mom had always gotten pregnant the first month, she bragged. So, I went to grad school. I had it all planned out. I would have a baby in May or June, right after graduation. We started trying in the fall. I timed my cycles so I'd have an idea of when I was ovulating, but we didn't worry too much about it. A month passed, then another, and another. After four months of trying, I knew. I can't tell you why. I am a nurse. I know they don't consider it infertility until you've been trying for a year. But I knew something was wrong. I felt it in my gut.

Let me back up. My husband had thyroid cancer. I guess he still does, but he's okay. He was diagnosed the year after we got married. He had a radical neck dissection and underwent two rounds of radioactive iodine. At that time, we asked questions about banking sperm, but they told us it wasn't necessary. Unlike chemo or radiation, radioactive iodine is specific to the thyroid and doesn't affect fertility. He also had varicocele. This is essentially varicose veins within the scrotum. It's super common. Usually it doesn't cause much of an issue so they don't do much about it. Most guys who have it are able to conceive, but a high number of guys who struggle with infertility have it.

So somehow, because of this history, I convinced my husband and his doctor to at least check a sample. After four months, which really is unheard of! I figured, maybe his counts were a little low or his swimmers were a little slow. I wasn't prepared for the result. Zero. Zilch. None. My husband had no sperm. Was it because of the cancer or the treatment? No one could really say. There wasn't a good reason for it. He was healthy, an athlete. They checked and rechecked the test, but the results were always the same. No sperm. So, they referred us to urology, but the first guy didn't really have any answers. So, he referred us to a more specialized urologist. He decided maybe it was because of the varicocele. There is a surgery to correct it so we decided to move forward with it. Usually you see results within a few months after the surgery. Three months later, no sperm.

Then they decided to do a specialized biopsy called a TESSA. This is essentially where they take a small piece of the testes, looking for sperm, in hopes of using it for IVF. My poor husband to this day will say this is the worst procedure EVER. It is done under local anesthesia so he was awake the whole time. They also told him the results while he was still in the procedure so I wasn't even with him. I will never forget the way his face looked when he got to recovery. Puffy eyes from tears, head shaking back and forth. They didn't find any. Not even any in partial phases of development. He would never be able to father a child, the doctor confirmed.

All of this took a good year or so from that first sample.

Were we upset? Of course. Did we grieve? Of course. But I can say I always had a sense of peace about it. This was the way it was. We didn't have to go through that prolonged period of waiting like some couples did. There was no maybe someday. We could never have children together. Even with the cancer, the unknown was the worst. Once you knew what you were facing, you could move forward with a plan.

Our options were adoption or sperm donation. We read blogs and books and talked to people who had been there. We eventually decided we wanted both. As a nurse, I had always been fascinated with the human body, and with that, the miracle of pregnancy. As much as I wanted a child, I also wanted to be pregnant. To join that sisterhood of women who could talk about what food they craved or how long their labor lasted. My husband was adamant that he didn't want to take this away from me. Although, of course, I never saw it that way. WE were unable to conceive. It was never a him vs. me.

Since we knew childbearing years are limited, we decided to proceed with sperm donation. We could always adopt later. It's crazy how IVF is totally accepted and sperm donation is completely taboo. When people found out they were shocked. "Isn't that just for lesbians?" "MY husband would NEVER agree to that." We tried not to let it bother us. Thankfully, our families were supportive.

We were referred to a specialist. They gave us a list of sperm banks. We narrowed it down to one in Michigan or Ohio and started reviewing possible donors. We tried to laugh about the absurdity of the whole thing. We limited it to donors with brown hair and eyes, like my husband. We looked for men with a similar education level and interests to him. We ruled out men who were too heavy or too short. We secretly joked that it would be amazing to pick a man of a different race, then act mortified upon delivery when our child's skin color was different from my husband's. There really aren't that many donors so surprisingly this process didn't take as long as you'd think. We picked our winner, a med student, and requested vials of sperm. Unfortunately, this donor had just gone through a limited supply so we instead purchased vials from our second choice, a master's prepared music teacher.

You would think this would be hard for us, but in reality, it helped. It helped us feel a little less like we were playing God. It helped us to feel that God was really in control. We scheduled our first IUI. Since they had no reason to believe I had any fertility problems, they said I could do it "naturally". Ironic, don't you think? I took an at home ovulation test and called when it was positive to schedule it. The procedure was painless, no worse than a pap smear. They warned me that it usually takes several months to get pregnant. They told me not to take a pregnancy test until I missed a period. Like I could wait for that? I took a test five days before my missed period. Positive. I woke my sleeping husband and we cried.

I had an uneventful pregnancy. No morning sickness. No crazy cravings. We decided to wait to find out sex. Our baby measured big, with a head greater than 97th percentile. So, when our due date came, and I wasn't in labor, they scheduled an induction. Our beautiful son was born a few hours later. He was perfect. An answer to prayer. He looked just like his daddy with his big brown eyes.

Story over? Nope! Just starting really. Fast forward a year-and-a-half. We knew we wanted more children. We knew we were interested in adoption. We always felt connected to children here in the U.S. so we started looking into domestic infant adoption. We were excited. Enter gut. That pesky gut. Something just didn't feel right. After much prayer and discussion, we decided to do another sperm donation. We had been storing some sperm from our previous donor in case of future pregnancies. I went off birth control to begin timing my cycles to prepare.

Then one day at work, my friend and I were talking about our cycles. I looked at my tracker on my phone and saw that I was five days late. My friend joked, "If it was anyone but you, I'd say you were pregnant." We laughed it off, but I decided to take a test the next day, since we planned to go out to celebrate my 30th birthday that evening. Positive. Wait. Hold up. What? My husband is sterile. I looked at the box of the test. Expired. That explained it. I went to the store and bought five unexpired tests. All positive. My husband and I were, to put it mildly, shocked. I didn't believe it. This wasn't possible. The doctors had made that perfectly clear.

But with God, all things are possible. I got my prenatal blood work. Everything was normal. "It's for real," the note from my OB said at the top of the labs. We dared to dream. Our children were going to be 27 months apart. We told our family and friends because it was such a miracle. My stomach began to swell to that bloated stage, where only you can really tell. I scheduled my first OB appointment. My husband came along. Everything was perfect until my OB couldn't find a heartbeat. "Not uncommon," he said. "It's early, and your uterus is retroverted (pointing toward the back)." He scheduled an ultrasound for the next day. I still didn't really believe I was pregnant.

So, when the ultrasound tech put that cool probe on my belly, and a tiny baby appeared, I began to sob. Two perfect arms, two legs. Miraculous. Beautiful. But no heartbeat. Our baby measured 9w3d and I was supposed to be 9w5d. Our baby had died two days earlier. My body didn't even know. The sobs took over. Why, God? Why? We were okay. We were at peace with not being able to have a biological child. Why would you give us this miracle and then take it away?

I couldn't walk into our nursery to put our toddler to bed. I couldn't look at the baby pictures on his wall. Sometimes I would think I was okay, then break down into tears at random times. My son pointing to my belly and saying baby was the worst. I would gently tell him the baby had gone bye-bye, break down into another round of sobs, and hold him a little tighter. My husband was a rock. He should have been bitter. Ticked off even. He was sad, but he held it together for me.

Weeks passed, and months, and slowly I began to heal. To forgive. To be at peace. And then I began to wonder. Does my husband have sperm now? He went to the doctor. Six million. Not a lot, but some! We began to hope. We were told to try for a few months. Months passed. A year. We decided to go back to the fertility specialist. He was excited. In 18 years of practice, he had never heard our story. He suggested we try IUI again, this time with my husband's sperm. But when I went in for the first procedure, his counts had dropped again. 400,000. The nurse suggested we bank now, in case we were considering IVF in the future. She told us they don't usually do IUI if counts are less than 1 million because it's unlikely to work. We met with the doctor who suggested my husband go on Clomid. That made us laugh because we thought it was only for women. Turns out in addition to causing ovulation in females, it has been shown to increase sperm production in males. Worth a try.

So that's where we are now. We have a healthy, opinionated, funny, food-loving 2 1/2-year-old. I carried my husband's child for 9 weeks, a child that everyone said wasn't possible. We have both my husband and my son's donor's sperm in storage. We are still open to adoption someday, especially from the foster system. We are unsure what the future of our family looks like, but we have a big God and trust Him fully. We choose hope.

Izzy's Story

I was brought up by older parents, who were old fashioned, and sex and death were taboo subjects. I was always a quiet kid, probably from ending up an only child and pretty much over protected, no doubt due to my mum's two miscarriages after me (one a boy at five months). I was never allowed a bike due to this increasingly dodgy and busy area, and to this day still can't ride one. We didn't have money, but we were happy. I can say for sure that my childhood was the best time of my life. My teens were okay, but my confidence dropped further due to being tall and a late developer. So, I was skinny and lanky, and also very spotty with acne on parts of the face and body so I always kept to myself and did not even think of boyfriends back then!!

When I got older and discovered alcohol, about 18 or 19, I had a boyfriend, as it was the first time I left my parents' flat and started living in bedsits and flats owned by mainly dodgy private landlords (another long story). But this was the beginning of my history of bad relationships. My first boyfriend started to hit me and his excuse was because I wasn't having sex with him. This led to our eventual split, but then I went to see a counsellor and this was when I was first diagnosed with suffering from anxiety. I was only 19. I also had counselling for a condition called vaginismus, which is something I'd never heard of (a psychological condition where fear prevents penetration as the muscles tighten involuntarily) so this knocked my self-esteem even more. Apparently only about 2 in 1,000 women suffer from this at some time in their lives.

A year-and-a-half of counselling, and then my next boyfriend. He was much nicer and it took me to 22 years of age until I lost my virginity! Not a lot of people believed me at the time. Not that I cared much. That boyfriend didn't last either as he wasn't well and ended up in the hospital. So as not to bore you, I won't go into all the details.

Basically, more crap relationships that didn't last, but it took me to age 27 when I finally became pregnant for the first time, a VERY premature ejaculation is all I can say! I never even had sex so it was a complete shock when I found out! And being the "father", he wasn't there for me during the pregnancy, for the stillbirth, or even the funeral. So, I guess you can say while I suffer from this for the rest of my life, he didn't care.

So, what happened was I found out at eight weeks that I was expecting so then I had to start really looking after myself, and I eventually left the punk band I was in during a tour to do so (I ended up with flu and felt awful). Well, as another cruel blow, at 34 weeks, I went for the usual routine scan and they couldn't find any heartbeat. This was also unexplained, but could've been the stress because my landlord made me move so he could refurbish the flat and I was up and down the stairs, carrying stuff (I had five folks helping, but it was still stressful). Three days later I found out that my baby had died. Also, the cord was twisted around the neck and shoulder (found this out after I'd given birth), and he was very underweight, but still no real reasons after the post mortem.

After losing my son, things got worse. Another few hopeless relationships and especially one that was the WORST. He ripped me and my mum off (her wedding rings went missing and were never found), killed my pets, committed fraud by forging my check book, even tried to do my mum's as I'd just become power of attorney that year. He even deliberately gave me an STD!

So, another few years of hopelessness and drinking to cope until I found my present boyfriend. I've been with him for over eight years now. It took a lot of courage to start trying again for babies. By this time, I was 33 going on 34, but, of course, after all my experiences of the past, we wanted to make sure we were right for each other. So, another two years of persuading passed, and finally I came off my long-term anti-depressants and started trying. And it takes A LOT of courage without my pills, and, of course, the courage needed to try for a baby again after all my experiences, especially the stillbirth.

And it took my doc about two years before she started helping us. The fact we don't live together or even in the same town doesn't help. She took blood samples, which told her I was still ovulating. More blood tests, urine tests, and semen tests. People say you must have fun trying. I DONT THINK SO! It's a nightmare, but so far everything was normal. The next test, a hydrotubation laparoscopy. A WHAT? I was worried and anxious all the time. It ruined our Christmas and New Year as I thought I was getting the test in January of 2008. Turned out it was just more blood and urine samples, etc. Then I had to wait until April for a pre-op health check. During all this, I'm still at college doing essays and case histories, visiting my only family, my mum with dementia in the nursing home, partner is working and we're STILL trying to conceive.

My test eventually comes through May 21, 2008. I somehow get through it, although the doc allowed me to take a valium the night before and on that morning (for my bad anxiety), as long as the anesthetist knows. Turns out, after all that, they couldn't find anything wrong. So, infertility is still left unexplained. So, we were told not to try anymore until a month after op and after my next period. So, no closure, and you grieve for the kids you could've had in the time you've been trying, the wasted years, and your future more and more as time goes by. It's ironic to think that I've been in my longest and best relationship ever, and we try and try and try, and it DOESN'T happen.

We stopped having sex for a long time as it turns into all about making babies and begins to be anxiety ridden, as after about the first or second year, you begin to wonder what is wrong. And every time my period comes, it's not just the cramps, but the debilitating depression and feelings of failure and inadequacy. And year after year it's the same. Another year gone by, watching kids while I sit alone in the park or down the beach, and wonder if a miracle is EVER going to happen for us.

Fast forward to May of 2010. I have started seeing a hypnotherapist, and also joined a gym to try to get more fit. In August of 2010, I feel I have tried so hard to make everything work, just to be gutted all over again. I need even more of a miracle for anything to work, and I really don't know what I'm going to do next, or what to do with my life. Will my life ever be happy again? I have had so much loss and pain and misery, and my partner isn't happy either, obviously. I feel like I'm letting him down. SIX years we've been at this! We got offered to do IUI, but it hasn't worked due to the eggs not maturing.

So, we were told the only option left was egg donation, but it's very complicated. I'm now on the waiting list for an egg. Could be over a year. I don't know how I'll get my head around this one now. It won't be my genes, and I feel I'm letting my parents down (even though they are no longer alive). But I feel I have to at least give my partner a chance to become a dad, even though, ironically, he's the one that isn't as bothered as me about being a parent.

Two years on from our failed IUI, I've just turned 44. We have now been told we are at the top of the waiting list for egg donation. We have been trying naturally again all that time. We've been given a list of eight egg donors to choose from that already have frozen eggs in bank, unless we wait on the next donor with fresh eggs, but we don't know how much longer that will take and what their characteristics will be. It's so confusing as who to choose, and I feel I'm going through it alone as my partner works away most of the week. We finally made a choice, though.

In October of 2012, everything was looking good. My partner gave a good sample although he was nervous, and the four donor eggs thawed okay. I got the embryo transfer, which went fine. I was so nervous beforehand. I met up with a friend who came with me and she kept my spirits up by joking all the way through! They put the best embryo in. I've still got two embryos being frozen, and the fourth one sadly was discarded as it stopped developing.

Well, after 16 years since the loss of my son at 34 weeks, and over eight years of unexplained infertility, I got a positive! It was VERY early days and I was afraid to believe it myself. I was so scared, and I was also aware that I don't want to upset those of my friends who are still going through infertility and still childless, as I know EXACTLY how painful it is for them to read about others' pregnancies, but I hope if they ARE reading this that I will NEVER forget my plight to get to this stage, which is a total miracle, and the fact I had to use donor eggs. I know it's not for everyone.

Well, after 8 months with only one major scare (I had some spotting at 23 weeks and had to stay overnight in the hospital), I was induced at 37 weeks (they did this because of my history). Our daughter was born on June 19, 2013, coming in at 6 pounds, 4 ounces! Our long-awaited miracle arrived at last!

In February of 2015, almost two years later, we tried for a sibling for our daughter with one of the frozen embryos from our previous treatment. I didn't want her to end up on her own like me. But sadly, this time it did not work, so we only had one embryo left.

It is now March 2017. Our last embryo worked! Our daughter got her sibling, a little

sister, who is now just over a year old. It wasn't an easy pregnancy, but I can't believe I got pregnant again at age 47! I will always grieve my firstborn, all the time lost, and the fact the genetic line ends with me, and also that I never made my parents grandparents while they were still alive, but I'm very lucky to have what I have now and am eternally grateful to those who donate their eggs.

Jennifer's Story

"Oh, you're married how long?" "Do you have kids?" Those are just some of the questions that I get. "Yes, just a four legged one," is the response that I give. "Well, when are you going to start having kids?" That is the one that always punches me in the gut. Like a semi-truck carrying 6,000 tons has just ran over my heart. If it was up to me, I would have had a child about 2 1/2 years ago. For some reason that I have still yet to figure out, God has had a different plan. For about 2 1/2 years now, me and my husband have been dealing with a huge white elephant in the room: infertility.

We have been blessed with a couple of best friends who have gone through the same thing. So, after sharing how we have been trying for about a year, I told my best friend. After an afternoon of tears, hugs, and understanding, she told me to make an appointment with my OB/GYN. So, we started round one of drugs. For a long time, we never told anyone what we have been going through (expect our friends). Well, all that was about to change. My mother-in-law works at our local pharmacy so I knew that maybe it was time. The first round of drugs I came in to pick up. I went into her office and told her everything. Let me tell you, it was like the world was lifted off my shoulders. Telling my parents was a different story. It was Father's Day and my lovely (with just a touch of sarcasm) sister-in-law has my niece with a shirt that says, "Big Sister," on it. All of a sudden it was like the Hoover Dam had opened up, because just like that, tears came.

After three months on hormone pills (Clomid and Femara) that didn't work and gave me nothing but hot flashes and headaches, it was time for the God-awful question to my husband. Once he got tested, we finally had answers. It felt like an answer to prayer. Our issue is that my husband has low sperm count and not only that, but low mobility. In English, that means his sperm don't move like they should.

The next step is to go through treatments, whether that means IUI, IVF, or even adoption. Treatments that I never thought in my entire life I would have to consider. I just have to remember two things. One, God can move mountains; and two, I will never sink with God holding me up.

I was that type of person who thought why would people get a tattoo. I mean, why would you put yourself through so much pain and mark up your body? I also never thought I would be going through infertility either. Now I have three tattoos. One is mountains with a cross and the words, "God can move mountains". It's to remind me that no matter what issue you may be struggling with, God can move any size mountain. My other one is an anchor with two hands holding it up as a reminder that I will never sink, not with my Savior holding me up. The last one is a cross with a greater sign and an arrow pointing up and down, just to remind me that God is greater than any ups or downs that I am going through.

I will say going through all this has taught me a few things. First, it has taught me how strong a marriage can be. One of my favorite quotes is as follows, "The couples that are meant to be are the ones who go through everything that is meant to tear them apart and come out even stronger than they were before." That was from the Huffington Post. I feel that quote sums up everything. The second thing that it taught me is not to judge anyone. I mean, you have no idea what they are going through in their day-to-day life. The third thing is to trust the Great Almighty. He already knows what my future may look like even though I don't and He has a plan for my life.

Joanne's Story

I'm 38 years old and I have three children. All three were born via C-section. When I was 22 1/2 weeks pregnant with my youngest daughter, I nearly died. I was rushed into the hospital as I had an umbilical hernia that got wrapped around my bowel. Luckily, I had emergency surgery, a temporary fix, and my baby was fine. I decided then that I didn't want more children. On my delivery date, it was arranged that they would do my section then sterilize me like I'd asked and then finish the hernia operation. After they delivered my baby, my husband took her back to the ward to wait for me. I started having second thoughts on being sterilized, but as my husband had gone back to the ward, it wasn't a decision I could make on my own without talking to him.

That day was both the best day of my life and then turned into what I thought was the worst day. I could no longer have a baby. My gut was telling me I had made the biggest mistake of my life. I went back to the ward at last to be with my baby girl. Days, weeks, months, and years later I was still hating myself for making the mistake. Then about seven years ago my husband said he'd like another baby. OMG! I felt like I'd won the lottery so we talked and talked more. I went to see my doctor about having the sterilization reversed. Turns out it wasn't possible. My heart sank. Turns out they had chopped my tubes and there was no way of reversing it.

We then spoke about IVF. My doctor referred us to a clinic. We spoke to the consultant and he said, yes, it would be possible, but I'd need to lose weight as you have to have a certain BMI. So, the diet began in July 2015. By January 2016 I'd done it! I'd hit my target weight the clinic set me! Yes, this is it! It's going to happen!

So, base line scans and blood tests began. I was then sent for a nurse consultation. She talked about the meds and how to take them, when to take them, etc. Wow, this is it! We're going to have our baby! I had chosen to do time-lapse imaging. This is where the eggs and sperm are put in a machine and watched closely, and it takes pictures every ten minutes. Then they put it on a USB stick and we have a video of our embryo. We were due to start our cycle March 2016. Then one day we got a call telling us not to start. My thyroid levels weren't right so we had to lower my dose bit by bit. July comes and we were told my levels were fine so I could start my meds. My period came and I started my meds. Wow, doing my first injection was so scary! We were starting our rollercoaster journey. I was both excited and so scared at the same time.

A week later we went for a scan to see how my eggs were reacting to the medication. Yes, everything's looking great! I have 38 follicles. Two days later I went back for another scan. YES! We were booked in for egg collection. Egg collection day came. I was a wreck. I didn't sleep the night before. Off we drove to the clinic again, excited and scared. Off I go to get ready. I was praying everything would go okay. I was called in. I get on the bed, my legs placed in stirrups, my dignity flown out the window as my male consultant sit at the bottom of my bed staring right up there, but I didn't mind. This was going to be worth it. I was sedated. 38 eggs collected. "Amazing," they told us.

Once I came around, I went home to await the call the following day to let us know how many eggs had fertilized. 15! Things were looking great. Day three comes. We get a call to say seven eggs are doing great, and they booked me in for egg transfer. Two days later, transfer day came. I'm sitting in the waiting room, drinking loads of water as I needed a full bladder. I'm called in and told what was going to happen, etc., and legs in stirrups again, and my little eggs have been transferred. Wow! At this moment in time I'm pregnant until proven otherwise. The two-week wait starts. I got to day five and just wanted to do a test. Negative. But I was still hopeful. After all, I had tested nine days too early.

Two days later I had the urge to test again and OMG! My BFP!! I was excited and emotional. I retested again, and again positive. I called the clinic and they said I have tested too early and to wait to day 14, but I couldn't. Every day for the next seven days I tested twice a day. This seems very surreal. Is this really happening? Am I having a baby? And by day 13 I called the clinic to let them know it's still positive. We have done it! We're having a baby!

I had to have a scan at seven weeks to confirm everything was good. Every day until scan day I was excited, but also in denial. Can I really be pregnant? Scan day came and there in the screen was my little bean and his heartbeat bumping away.

Then the following day my heart stopped. Just after lunch I got up off the sofa and blood ran down my legs. I screamed! I called my doctors and was told to get to the hospital. I called an ambulance. Still gushing blood, I was rushed to the hospital. After waiting hours, and, yes, it was hours, I was examined. They pulled a huge clot out that was about the size of my hands. I'm still crying here, thinking my baby has gone. I couldn't get a scan until the following day. That night was awful. Then I was called for my scan. I cried and cried on my way down, the porter must have thought I was crazy. I went for my scan, and there on the screen was my baby! I couldn't see the screen through the tears. I was told to rest once I got home. My husband wouldn't let me do anything. We had to protect this baby.

I bled for weeks, but had weekly scans and all was okay. Weeks went by and I went to see my doctor. I had a bad discharge. I knew it wasn't thrush and it didn't smell or itch. She said she'd do a swab. It then came back I had group b strep. May I say they don't test for it routinely here in the U.K.? She'd spoken to two consultants about treatment, but both advised it didn't need treating until labor, but as I was doing a C-section, I didn't need to worry. I'd never heard of this group b strep so came home and researched it. I went back to my doctor who sent me to the midwife as I was a high-risk pregnancy. I went to see the consultant at the hospital who advised miscarriage is very rare and not to worry.

I went back at 12 weeks and had a scan, and baby was doing great, jumping away so they found it hard to get all his measurements. We then went back at 16 weeks. Everything seemed okay until they couldn't find his heartbeat. My heart stopped. Then they scanned me and baby was fine. Turns out my placenta was at the front. Two days later on my oldest child's 18th birthday, I went for a private gender scan as I couldn't wait to find out team blue or team pink, but we never found out as my little monkey had his legs crossed and wouldn't let us see. I was booked to go back the following week.

Three days later my husband was off, out shopping, and asked if I wanted to get out of the house. I'd been on bed rest for weeks and only going out to doctors and hospital appointments. I went to the loo. As I walked away from the loo, I had fluid running down my legs. I screamed. I called the hospital who advised me to go straight up. My husband drove like a mad man. I'm trying not to move as every move made the fluid leak more, but deep down I knew it was my waters.

Once on the labor ward, three doctors scanned me and confirmed my baby had died. Now this was the worst day of my life. I cried and screamed! After a while I was told they would leave me to start contractions. If nothing after 48 hours, they would give me meds to start this. I was put in a side room, a beautiful room. It was for mums who had lost their babies. That night I didn't sleep. I cried all night. The following day they came in and did my blood pressure and temp, etc., and all was fine.

Then 20 mins later I started shaking like I was so cold. I couldn't stop. I buzzed for the nurse and then don't really remember much. I very vaguely remember them trying to but a PICC line in my arm. Turns out I had septicemia. I was very ill. I have flash backs and am told bits by my husband and the midwife, but they gave me tablets to get me to deliver my baby. I remember some of the contractions and my baby boy was born at 7:15 p.m. on 10/24/2016. He weighed 80 grams. He was so small and perfect.

I was told after that, that the tests on the placenta showed it was the group b strep that killed my baby boy. They have said if I'm lucky enough to get pregnant again via IVF and I do get group b strep again, they will treat. Well, they should have treated me this time and my baby would have been born via C-section on March 28, 2017. I'm now waiting to start IVF again. Nothing will replace my baby boy. I visit his grave a lot, and now have also recently been diagnosed with PTSD.

Kari's Story

My high school sweetheart and I got married in 2007 after seven years of dating. We were just so excited to be married that we really weren't in any rush to start a family. We spent about five years just enjoying married life and basically doing whatever we wanted whenever we wanted. We spent a lot of time with friends and taking trips, as well as eating out and staying up late if we wanted to. Sometimes I wondered if I would ever want children. We were so happy just the two of us.

One thing I was becoming bothered by, however, was the fact that I was rapidly gaining weight. Our lifestyle was not the healthiest, and grocery shopping used to consist of the cheapest processed foods we could get, or eating out because it was fun and easy. I gained somewhere around 40 pounds within the first seven or so years of marriage and was completely unhappy with how I looked and felt. I was also completely fatigued most of my life. I had been this way since puberty. Naps where generally two to three hours long after school or work and left me feeling groggier afterward. I also had always had irregular periods, and my doctor suggested putting me on birth control to regulate it from the age of 16. I never worried too much about it after that.

I sought out advice from an OB/GYN around the age of 24. The appointment was quick and I left feeling like she had dismissed my concerns. I was getting used to this since doctors seem to always respond the same. "Just take birth control to regulate your cycles and it will be fine." I asked this OB/GYN what would happen when we wanted to actually have children. "Oh, you will be fine. You might just need a little help getting you to ovulate with some fertility medication." She made it sound like absolutely nothing to worry about.

Eventually we did decide that it would be best for me to get off birth control and see what happened. I wondered if it was the cause of my weight gain, and also, we were feeling more ready to start a family. The symptoms quickly worsened. The weight kept packing on and did not respond to any short-lived dieting efforts. I would get frustrated and give up. I started growing dark and coarse hairs on my chin which also was difficult for my self-esteem. I also felt alone because I didn't know anyone else who experienced this at my age. The fatigue was becoming more intense. After I started my first serious job, I would come home after a work day and crash on the couch for three hours. I'd wake up feeling terrible and even depressed.

The depression is what finally led me to get a second opinion. This time I took my husband with me in hopes that I would not get dismissed immediately. To my relief, within the first five minutes of sitting down with me and hearing my symptoms, she diagnosed me with polycystic ovarian syndrome. I was happy to have an answer, but was a bit in shock about everything that it meant. It sounded complicated and it was something that was incurable. Even the doctor did not know the cause. She proceeded to give me a lot of overwhelming information and suggested that I see a nutritionist because it sounded as though I was going to need to transform virtually everything about the way I ate. Also, she did not beat around the bush about the fact that infertility is a very common symptom.

Of course, when I went home I did nothing but research PCOS. It was scary. There was so much conflicting information out there and such a laundry list of other symptoms that can develop as well as several other serious diseases you are at higher risk for such as diabetes, non-alcoholic fatty liver disease, ovarian cancer, heart disease, and many others. Again, the depression started setting in, now with some added anxiety and panic attacks. The day I was diagnosed, I felt so good to have an answer that I forgot that the answer may be so difficult to swallow.

I tried with all my might to talk myself out of feeling hopeless, but it was no use. To add insult to injury, I had read that PCOS often is the cause of anxiety and depression because of all the hormone imbalances involved. I was beginning to hate this syndrome that I had never even heard of before. Instead of attacking the symptoms with cutting the necessary things out of my diet and exercising five times a week and seeing a nutritionist, I chose denial instead. I kept researching the suggestions, but didn't know which ones to take so instead I just didn't try.

Sometime later, after gaining some control of the depression, my husband and I became more serious about having kids. It was obvious that it was not going to happen on our own. I had now been off of birth control for nearly four years and never had so much as a positive pregnancy test. I had heard so much about Clomid and my doctor finally referred me to an OB/GYN that would prescribe it to me. I remember being so thrilled that we were starting this. I had been told and read so many hopeful stories about Clomid being "the miracle drug". We were told we could do three rounds of Clomid with timed intercourse through this OB office. In my mind, I was convinced that I would be pregnant within those three months. I wasn't.

Blown away with the disappointment and being more confused than ever, we were referred to an infertility specialist. We felt so casual about getting pregnant in the beginning of this process and now our desire to have a child was growing by the day. I finally realized that this was going to be hard. We would need more than just "a little help". I did begin to make some healthier choices during this time and was actually able to find a formula of eating that allowed me to shed a few pounds. My husband and I trained for a 5K and were able to make jogging a regular way to exercise in the spring and summer months. This was a large accomplishment for me because I never thought I would willingly run for exercise. It became a way to prove to myself that I could make healthy changes on my own.

When we finally had our first appointment at the fertility center, I remember sitting down with the doctor and hearing that I had not even so much as ovulated with the Clomid cycles. I couldn't believe it. This medication did not even get us any closer to a baby than trying on our own. Now we were feeling pretty defeated as well as broke. We were not prepared for the financial aspect of this, but felt so strongly the need to continue. During this time, I became somewhat obsessed with daydreaming about getting pregnant and having a baby.

We tried several medicated cycles through the fertility center and then moved on to IUI. Each cycle was a mixed bag of emotions. I started feeling like I was on an endless cycle and my emotions were dictated by where I was in the cycle. There would be some excitement for each new cycle, and it felt like we would have so much hope that this would be the time. I really tried to eat the right things and doing the right things. I limited sugar and caffeine. I was so motivated to do everything that I could to make it work. Then during the two-week wait, the time would crawl. As we neared the end of it, I would start to get irritable and anxious feeling like I was preparing for a punch to the gut. Although it was so easy to be hopeful in the beginning, as we would near during testing time, I couldn't help but prepare for the worst. I didn't want to disappoint people. I didn't want to see the look of disappointment on my husband's face again. I didn't know how I could handle looking at another negative test. Over a year of working with the fertility center, we experienced nine unsuccessful cycles.

With each negative test, we would feel deflated. I would feel like I couldn't go on trying. It was too difficult to have hope and be let down each time. I really relied on my support system during this time. My mom, my sister-in-law, a couple of close friends, and a few co-workers, knew in depth what I was going through. They were the ones who rode the emotional rollercoaster with us. They were the ones in our corner who helped us have hope when we had none. They were flexible with us when we had to miss work for appointments or had to miss outings due to medication schedules or ultrasounds.

Eventually our support system grew as I decided to attend a local infertility support group called Hopeful Hearts. The flyer for the group was hanging at the fertility center. The group was held in a church a mile away from where I worked. We began attending that church every Sunday and finding a place that felt like home in the midst of everything. I was able to connect with other ladies in the support group as well as in the church who had experienced the heartbreak that we had. My husband was able to talk with other men who knew all too well the struggle that we faced, and it helped us realize we were not alone.

We had to take a couple breaks in between cycles and I would be so reluctant to do it, but then I would enjoy life so much more during the breaks. I would lose track of the date or where I was in my cycle. I felt more free. I learned to let acceptance of our situation slowly creep in. I stopped pinning nursery themes and making baby registry lists. I stopped imagining about someday and slowly started living for the present. I started to focus on all of the things that I had in my life and stopped focusing so much attention on the one thing I did not have.

My relationship with my husband has grown an incredible amount through this experience. We learned to value things we were overlooking before. We started realizing that just he and I and our dog were still a family unit full of so much love. We have grown in our spiritual lives and learned to accept the life we have and to lean on the power of prayer. We were able to be vulnerable with our friends and find out who was willing to stick with us through this journey. So many of our friends not only stuck around, but asked how we were doing and lent an empathetic ear rather than random advice.

At this point, my husband and I still very much long for children, but we have to take a break from fertility treatment due to the financial and emotional burden of it all. We have decided to take a trip to Ireland to celebrate our 10th wedding anniversary. This is sort of out of our comfort zone and seemed like a strange decision since we were feeling so financially strapped. But we both felt this was something that we needed to do. We need to enjoy the state of life that we are in, never knowing what life is going to bring next. We have entertained the possibilities of adoption or further procedures at the fertility center, but it doesn't seem to be the right time in our lives for either of these things right now. We both realize that we have endured some tough years and that it is time to start healing from the ache that has dominated our hearts for so long.

We remain hopeful that the desires of our hearts will be met and someday our family will expand. But right now, we are just going to live in joy and gratitude, for everything and everyone we have around us. And we are still watching and waiting for that miracle on the horizon.

Kris' Story

We got married in 1982 and wanted children right away, but I was in the Army and having extremely irregular menses. I could go for months with nothing, and have months of bleeding daily. I was put on "the pill" to try to control the bleeding. Then a couple of months later the next doctor said the pill was causing the bleeding and I needed another method of birth control. It was a very frustrating period of time.

After discharge from the Army and three years of trying to conceive, I underwent a laparoscopy in a German hospital. There was no physical reason found for my failure to get pregnant. Hubby also underwent testing and was found fertile. We then went on Clomid to stimulate ovulation. During this time, I avoided situations where I would see babies as much as possible, and never bought anything in the baby care section of the store. If that was the only place to get something we needed, I would go to another store or do without. Mother's Day was a near nightmare for me, and I would stay home alone if at all possible.

After more than a year on Clomid, I was in my kitchen the day before Thanksgiving of 1986 and started to hemorrhage. The bleeding and clotting was so severe that I barely made it around the corner to the powder bathroom and sit down on the toilet. I sat there for an hour until hubby came home to take me to the ER. This was before cell phones, and I was too weak to get up and walk to the telephone. At the ER, they did a pregnancy test and said I was pregnant, but they couldn't explain what the bleeding implications were. They made an appointment for me the following Monday at an OB/GYN. On Monday I was told it was a false positive and I was not, and probably never would be, pregnant. In December, we started the process to become foster parents.

In February of 1987 (yes, just two months later), I was told I was five months pregnant. No explanation for the hemorrhage episode was ever given, nor was an explanation why the OB examined me at three months' gestation and told me I was NOT pregnant. In March, we were asked to take in two foster girls, sisters just turned four and five, even though our license was not approved yet (the state was desperate for a home for these two girls together). In April, I went into pre-term labor and gave birth at 28 weeks' gestation to a boy, 2 pounds 13 ounces. He spent eight weeks in the hospital, but came home with no special equipment. After quite a few medical complications, he did grow up to be a special needs adult, just mildly handicapped, with Asperger's Spectrum Disorder.

When the oldest was 18 months old we went back on Clomid and conceived after three months. This time I moved in with my parents since my hubby was being sent to school and then transferred to Germany during this pregnancy. I was on modified bed rest to avoid another pre-term delivery, and it worked! A healthy, full-term boy at 9 pounds 10 ounces was delivered after a couple of scares around the 28-week gestational mark. When he was two months old, we moved to Germany to reunite the family. We figured our family was complete and did not resume fertility drugs, assuming that no drugs meant no further pregnancy, since bed rest with two young boys would be near impossible without help.

God has a sense of humor, but He also loves me, and we conceived without medication. Since son number two was a large full-term child, we assumed no bed rest would be necessary for number three. We were wrong. Our third son was born at 29 weeks' gestation after a week in the hospital trying to hold off labor, weighing in at 2 pounds 3 ounces. He presented breech so we chose a C-section with sterilization at that time. We were unwilling to risk another extreme preemie. I am very grateful that I learned to speak German and had our first preemie in an American hospital so, when the terminology based on Latin and Greek words was used, I was able to understand. He spent 10 weeks in the hospital and came home on O2 monitors.

Our boys are all grown up now. One is married and has a daughter of his own. We are very blessed, but will never forget those years of heartache.

Laura's Story

I think I'll just start by telling you our story. I'll try to stick to the facts, with a bit of the emotions that have gone with our journey. A warning up front. I have not come out the other side yet (emotionally speaking). I have been honest in here, and I don't mean to offend you at all. Perhaps you have had different emotions during this time. I pray God will use even a fraction of this to help you in some way.

First off, you are definitely not alone. Many couples struggle with infertility. And even though many people are struggling with infertility, it is a very lonely disease. I often felt (and sometimes still feel) deep feelings of loneliness, as though we were the only ones going through this. In a way, it is a very personal thing and can be very isolating. It's not something people freely share with just anyone and that also contributes to feeling alone. Anyway, when we started trying, I had no idea that infertility was this common.

We started TTC in August of 2007. My husband was in his second to last year of residency, not making much money, and since we knew I would be staying home, we weren't comfortable with having a baby any earlier because of finances. Anyway, we started trying. Honestly, before this point, I had never paid much attention to my cycles. I had a period every month, and while I would sometimes bleed for up to 10 days, I thought nothing of it until we had been TTC for six months without success. Then I started charting: temperatures, ovulation signs and symptoms, cycle starting and ending date, etc. I realized I was all over the place. Nothing was consistent.

So, I went to see my family doc. She ran some blood tests, which showed some imbalance in my hormones. She diagnosed me with PCOS, even though I had none of the other symptoms associated with this disease. With PCOS, ovulation can be irregular and/or absent all together. So, I bought a ton of ovulation predictor strips and around day 14 of every month I was peeing on a stick. (Not a pregnancy test stick, but an ovulation test strip. Yet another depressing point for me.)

We continued TTC. Nothing. My emotions were all over the place. Anger, sadness, jealousy, envy, depression, worthlessness. Every day I was asking God why. Many of our friends were announcing pregnancies or second pregnancies. And we still, after a year of trying, were not pregnant. More than that, the spontaneity and intimacy was gone. It wasn't fun anymore, and we were living in two-week waiting periods. Wait two weeks for ovulation. Wait two weeks to see if we were pregnant. Only to find out we had to go through it all over again the next month. It was exhausting and very, very frustrating.

We decided to go see a fertility doctor, a RE. I'm not sure exactly when our visits with him started, but he ran some tests on both of us. In our case, we both contribute to our infertility. The doctor put me on a drug called Clomid, a very popular drug for PCOS, which helped to regulate my ovulation.

Not only did our RE recommend tests and Clomid, but he

recommended we try intrauterine insemination. We had deep discussions about this, especially if we agreed with it ethically. We felt that Clomid and IUI were acceptable, since we were simply increasing the odds of getting pregnant by otherwise natural means. We did four IUIs. This procedure did not hurt at all. It was just a nuisance. In my opinion, we should have just been able to get pregnant the normal, fun way. Not with a tube, a donation into a cup, and a doctor. The IUIs were worth a shot (clearly, we tried it four times), but were not successful. And along with each try we had more waiting, uncertainty, and frustration.

Finally, our RE said the next step would be IVF. We asked about more drugs for me, or different drugs, or drugs for my husband to help him with his problem. No more decent options there. I was now ovulating on schedule with the Clomid, and there was nothing they could give to my husband. IVF was the only other option, for us anyway. It was at this point we had another heart-to-heart discussion. We felt that we could put the IVF money towards a procedure with no guarantees, or we could put that money towards adoption: a guarantee that we would be parents, at least someday. Needless to say, we decided to adopt.

Some background. Many, many years before any of this, before we were even married, my then boyfriend and I talked about what our family might look like some day. We both independently said that, while we would like to have biological children, we also wanted to adopt. We knew we would have the means to adopt, but we also knew that we would have the love and acceptance that goes into adopting a child.

Now back to the timeline. IVF or adoption. It was an easy choice. We had wanted to adopt anyway, and while we never imagined it would be for our first child, it was an easy step for us to take. So, in February of 2009, we attended an orientation for Bethany Christian Services' domestic infant adoption program. We came away from that meeting not only ready to sign up, but also ready to adopt transracially, if that was God's plan. We filled out all the necessary paperwork, became an approved, waiting family by the end of June 2009, and then we waited.

We had several expectant moms and couples view our profile at Bethany. In October 2009, we were chosen by an expecting couple. Mom was white. Dad was black. We met them, were "matched", got to know them, took them to a couple appointments, and were planning on being there for the baby's birth, due sometime around December 22. Sometime around thanksgiving, though, we had a sense this couple wanted to parent their baby. Of course, we were okay with this. This boy wasn't ours yet and they had every right to change their minds. Problem was, they weren't saying anything. But I could tell they were no longer committed to their adoption plan.

Our social worker went to see them shortly after we expressed our concerns. Sure enough, they admitted that they had changed their minds and wanted to try to parent. This may seem very sad and it was sad in a way. But more so, it was a relief! We knew they weren't in it 100% and, quite frankly, we couldn't see ourselves with this baby if they didn't want that. Phew! So, our match became a failed match. That was December 3, 2009. And on December 6, 2009, our son was born! We drove down the next morning to meet him and instantly were his parents. I say this because the moment we arrived at the hospital nursery, they wheeled him, along with a bottle, in and said, "He's ready to eat." We fed him and then they gave us a family room. We all stayed the night together at the hospital. The next afternoon we signed some papers at Bethany and then drove three hours back home with our new son sleeping soundly in the back seat.

His birth mom signed over her parental rights on December 23 and we finalized his adoption on July 22 of 2010. While I still struggle with my emotions connected to our infertility (it has gotten less with time), I also realize that if things had gone according to plan, we would not be the parents of this incredible, little boy. It's hard for me to imagine that. And while being his mom has been wonderful and I wouldn't change anything that has happened, his presence in our lives will never change the fact that we went through an incredible time of suffering in our marriage/life. It will never make it "all better". Being a mom to this boy helps, but I will never be the same person I was before infertility. It has changed me forever and not even a six-pound, beautiful, brown-skinned, happy baby boy can fix me, nor should he be expected to.

I hesitate to tell you that I am still very much on a journey of healing. I think some of our family members thought that by becoming parents we would be healed, we would get over the sad and just move on. I had to educate them that adopting doesn't change the fact that we are still infertile, that we still went through a very challenging and sad time.

Through all of this, God is molding me and teaching me. I have gone along with his plan kicking and screaming a lot of the time, but I know it is all for His divine purpose to take shape in my life. And now I know more about infertility and adoption then I ever imagined, and I have a heart for those going through both.

Lauren's Story

I'm not sure if my story would be encouraging or not to those who are currently struggling with infertility, but I did struggle with it myself. I was trying to get pregnant for over a year-and-a-half and my doctor simply labeled it as infertility. He said they almost never tell a couple that it's impossible to get pregnant, but that their chances of getting pregnant could simply be lower than normal. Thankfully, we did eventually get pregnant and are expecting our first child in just three-and-a-half months! I don't know if I could go through the emotional stress of trying again for a second child since it took us so long on the first and I'm in my mid-30s, but I can definitely say that while we were trying, I felt incomplete, like I wasn't really a woman since I couldn't conceive, which is something that all women should be able to do. Going through that time of trying and being unsuccessful was one of the toughest things I have had to face personally.

Linda's Story

For as long as I can remember, I wanted to be a mother. As I got older, I thought I might like to be a teacher, but in the bottom of my heart, my longing to be a mother was the strongest. When I got married, we made a plan. My husband had three years of college to complete so we decided to wait two years before trying to have a baby. At the time, we had two other couples who were very good friends of ours. On New Year's Eve, 1975, the men all made a toast, "To our wives: may they all be pregnant by this time next year!" During that year, first one friend became pregnant, and by the end of the year, the other friend became pregnant, but we were still waiting and trying.

In early 1976, we decided to see our family doctor about our difficulty in getting pregnant within a year-and-a-half of trying. He told us to, "Relax. These things will happen in their own time." I remember thinking, how am I supposed to relax when this is something I want so badly, but it's not happening!

In the summer of 1976, we took a job in another state and began the process of finding out why I was not getting pregnant. We saw an OB/GYN who put me on a fertility drug. I was told to take my temperature every morning, and we started hoping again. During this time, my sister phoned with the happy news that she was pregnant. She had just gotten married, and although I was happy for her, the news hurt me. I also experienced feelings of jealousy. Why was it so easy for everyone else to conceive and so difficult for me? What was wrong with me?

In 1977, we moved back home so my husband could go back to school. Again, I saw a specialist. He wanted to start over with all the tests I had already had so he could come to his own conclusions. This put us back a year as far as I was concerned, and that was very frustrating for me. I again took the fertility drugs and felt my hopes climb. There were some months when I would be a few days, or even weeks late, and then my hopes would crash when it became obvious that I was not pregnant. This was a hard time for me. I experienced depression because I felt we would never have a family. I experienced envy when my sister became pregnant with her second child. My friends were also getting pregnant, and it was becoming harder to feel genuine happiness for them instead of jealousy. It seemed as though everyone was able to start a family except for us.

The more I learned about the reproductive process, the more I was convinced how complicated it really was. I was actually amazed that anyone was able to have a baby! A few years after this, I was sent off to yet another specialist in a bigger city, and he ran a few other tests. By now we were considering moving again.

One morning I was in the kitchen and had the 700 Club on our TV. I was half listening as I was doing the dishes when I heard Pat Robertson pray for a woman who had been trying for years to have a baby, and just like Abraham's wife, Sarah, God was saying her desire would be fulfilled at just the right time. I believed that promise was for me. And I prayed right there that, "God, please, give us a child when the time was right."

We did move a year later, and in that new place, another doctor wanted to start at the beginning, but this time we were both checked out for various things. By this time my sister had her third child, but even though it still hurt that she was able to conceive so easily and I couldn't, I hung on to the promise that I, too, would have a child. About this time, we also began to look at adoption, exploring all our options.

One afternoon, I came home from a horseback riding lesson, and my husband met me at the door. He said, "Guess what? You're pregnant!" I remember being shocked and saying, "You're kidding!" We had been at a wedding a few weeks before this and I remember telling my grandma about wanting a child, and she laughed and said, "Well, I guess hope springs eternal!" I mean, we had been married for nine years already. I felt like my chances were getting slimmer the older I got. And now, finally, I was going to have a baby!

So even though my story has a happy ending, I do remember the difficulty of trying to be happy for everyone else who was starting their own families. I remember the feelings of failure and depression each month when I saw the proof that I was not pregnant. I remember the feelings of frustration when well-meaning people would give unsolicited advice such as, "Relax," or, "Have you tried..." and then go on to list a number of things, or even to say, "Well, you can always adopt." Of course, this last one would always be followed by a story of someone who had adopted and then had gotten pregnant, proof in their minds of the validity of the advice to, "Relax," and, "Just don't think about it so much!"

I remember at times just simply feeling sorry for myself. I understand now that it was truly in God's right time. We had our first child when my husband was out of school, had a good full-time job, we had our house, and I no longer had to be the breadwinner. It was just the right time to start a family.

I also understand that there will be those who will never experience having their own family to raise. And I believe in time that God will replace that desire with something else that satisfies.

In the end, it is God who opens and closes the womb. But for a woman who struggles with infertility, it is also a rollercoaster that can take a toll on a relationship. Sex on demand is not all it's cracked up to be! It can be a stressful time for a couple, and often one partner wants this more than the other, which can also create stress. There are often financial burdens that go along with infertility and not everyone has a good insurance plan that will cover the extra expenses. Infertility is a difficult road to travel, and not everyone gets a happy ending.

The lesson I learned was that, ultimately, I was not the one in control even when this particular thing seemed so easy for everyone else. I learned to depend on God for patience. I learned to be thankful in every circumstance and to trust Him to know what was best for me. Psalm 37:4 - "Delight yourself in the Lord, and He will give you the desires of your heart!"

Lindsey's Story

*Lindsey actually has a blog called <u>By Grace the Roberts</u>. She has given me permission to use the information from her blog, which you can find the link to at the back of this book. Please check it out for more information.

My husband and I (high school sweethearts) found out we were pregnant with our first baby just a week before our one-year anniversary. Our hearts were filled with such joy with the expectation of our child. Sadly, we lost our first baby to miscarriage.

At this point, we knew we really wanted a child, so following doctor's approval, we skipped a month and tried the next cycle. We conceived the first time and were blown away by our miracle! Knowing how rare two miscarriages in a row are, we quickly created an announcement video (which was only to share with immediate family). Before we even had the chance to share, we unfortunately had to rush to the ER where we were told those dreaded words, "You are having another miscarriage." We were stuck hours from home that week, and I remained locked in a dark room filled with grief for my son; I think of it as my prison cell.

We decided to take some time off, and three months later found out we were expecting again! It came as a surprise! We approached this pregnancy with caution, but again the words rang in my head, "Three consecutive miscarriages is so rare! You will be okay!" Time passed and the thoughts and fear began to settle. I was filled with hope as I made it further along than the previous pregnancies, until it began to happen. I was all too familiar with what was happening. We laid our dear son to rest on our farm.

At this point, we finally qualified for testing. They found "nothing" wrong. We tentatively began trying again because, well, nothing was wrong. One year ago, almost to the day, we found out we were expecting our precious daughter. We were over the moon and filled with joy. That day we were completely snowed in on our farm! I couldn't wait to get off and get into the doctor to make sure everything was all right. I got my bloodwork back. Definitely pregnant, but progesterone was dangerously low.

After my second draw, I received the dreaded news, "Your levels dropped; you will begin miscarrying soon." Heartbroken and worn, we were finally sent to an RE where they performed extensive testing and treatments. One year later, we are still not pregnant. Our battle has shifted from carrying to term to getting pregnant.

Money is hard. My husband is in seminary and is a pastoral intern at our church, and I am a preschool teacher as well as work for the church. After we take some time off, we will be excited to try this new product I found called Stork. It's found in Walgreens in the family planning section next to the ovulation kits! Since each visit to the RE is incredibly expensive, I am looking forward to an option I can do safely from my home. It has been a long road for sure. We will be taking a half year break, and while it is hard to come to terms with, I know it will be a good re-set to my body.

Meghan Swann's Story

*Meghan has requested her full name be used because she is entering the publishing world. Though there is nothing to link her to right now, be on the lookout for her works!

January 6, 2006, was the day we officially decided to toss all the birth control pills and start our family. We had been married for two-and-a-half years by now so it seemed like a good time to start. I was told time and again how my family is full of "fertile myrtles" and how I would be pregnant in no time. I was technically pregnant all right. Chemical pregnancy number one of five happened shortly after.

As the months went on and no baby was growing in my uterus, I began to question my fertility status. Off to the first doctor of many, my gynecologist. I was given the first of many diagnoses, PCOS. I was told to take Metformin, and if I was not pregnant in three months, he would prescribe Clomid. I went home and bawled. Who takes pills to get pregnant? No one in MY family. PCOS was a bigger fear, though. Google was not my friend that night. Thankfully, I had stumbled across a trying to conceive forum in my PCOS search, and after reading for many months, I posted for the first time and connected with a group of ladies who supported me in more ways than just infertility battles. To this day, over 11 years later, 10 of us still regularly chat, and our lives have evolved from trying for our own babies to some welcoming grandbabies!

Over time, I would bounce back and forth between the many treatment options eastern medicine offered and taking breaks to try western medicine treatment options. Everything from acupuncture, moon phases, herbal concoctions, fertility monitors, dietary changes, shots, pills, and IUIs were tried. I had every test available run on me. Some multiple times. While I was told my fallopian tubes were open, my ovaries were aging, and had diminished ovarian reserve. I was told I had a hostile uterus that was killing the sperm before they could reach an egg to fertilize. I was in my early 20s. How was that possible?! I charted my basal body temperature and kept tract of my cervical mucous and cervical position. I *knew* my body. PCOS. Thyroid. Weight. It all was blamed at one time or another on our journey. I saw four different Reproductive Endocrinologists. Numerous OB/GYNs who "specialized" in reproductive health problems.

The many family members and friends who got pregnant while we tried was difficult to cope with. Some petty things like wanting to give our parents their first grand baby, but despite starting to try years prior, others "won" out.

My husband was tested several times. He got the gold star of perfection. It was all me. I became desperate. I begged my husband to just go sleep with another woman and have her agree to let me be the baby's mama. I didn't care how the baby came, as long as I was a mommy. We talked adoption. We discussed surrogacy. We had friends approach us to be our surrogates. We talked living as DINKs (dual income no kids). And then we decided to give IVF a try. We saw the top RE with the best success rates and did some additional testing and retesting. We had our timeline set. All we were waiting on to begin was my period to arrive.

It didn't arrive until sometime later, though. I was pregnant with our beautiful daughter. 4 years, one month, 17 days we tried to get pregnant. God carried us through the trials. He promised us that He wouldn't abandon us, and looking back, I can clearly see when He was holding me.

A little encouragement. I am now mom to three beautiful children. We did not have secondary infertility as defined by trying to conceive for 12 months or longer, as our second "only" took seven months of trying, and our third, eight months. The wounds infertility left have healed, but the scars remain that are forever there to remind me of our infertility journey. I'll always be open to give encouragement to those on the journey to parenthood because of my own infertility journey. You do not walk this path alone. From one sister to another, take encouragement!

Rachel's Story

My husband and I have been together for nearly 18 years. He's wonderful and I'm so blessed to have him by my side. He worked his tail off to put me through PT school over the course of eight years, with the goal being that we would have a better life to provide to our future children. I graduated in 2013 with my degree, and then it was FINALLY baby time!

We started trying right away. It was pretty fun until we got about six months in with no luck. I was 32 and he was 34 so we didn't feel as if time was on our side. We started with our OB and both underwent basic tests. My husband tested perfectly, and I was told that I ovulate irregularly. I was put on Clomid, and trying to conceive became exciting again! We just knew this would work for us.

We went through six cycles of Clomid, timed intercourse, and did ultrasounds without even a hint of a positive pregnancy test. I started to feel quite nervous about everything. All we have ever wanted was to become parents. I quickly discovered that infertility coverage was not part of our insurance, and that everything related to seeing a fertility specialist would be out of pocket. My student loan balance wouldn't allow us to consider taking out a loan for this process. I started asking around and found out from a friend that the state of Illinois mandated infertility coverage. That's when I made the decision to seriously consider moving away from all we have ever known for the chance to reach our ultimate dream of parenthood.

Fast forward six months and we made the move to Illinois from Missouri. My husband was incredibly supportive, and I found an employer that offered the coverage we needed. My supervisor was very receptive to our plans to become parents, which was much appreciated and put me at ease. From what I understand, not all employers are supportive. We met with the reproductive endocrinologist, then began months of tests and procedures. We ended up trying several more months of timed cycles with Femara before moving on to IUI. That was also unsuccessful and we were devastated. As usual, we were again met with the disappointment of failure. I was quickly approaching 35 years old and the clock just kept ticking louder each cycle. It was time to move on to IVF.

We began the IVF process and I was so overwhelmed!! It actually went by pretty quickly, and my specialist and nurses were phenomenal. The two-week wait was the worst one yet, but it ended with a wonderful blessing. The line was finally there! The beautiful, mythical, second pink line had arrived and it was ours! WE WERE PREGNANT! Three long years later we were finally expecting our first child and we couldn't have been any happier if we tried. I ended up taking 47 more of those tests. I loved seeing that line so much, and needed to rid myself of the pregnancy tests I had collected over the years, of course.

I made it to week twelve and breathed a sigh of relief. We made it through the "scary phase". We announced our immense joy with a special photo and poem we had planned for quite some time, and it finally felt real. I went in a few weeks later for genetic testing and a NT scan I had requested. In an instant, the overwhelming joy in my heart was replaced with pure devastation. Our baby did not develop normally and would not survive. It was a severe case of amniotic band syndrome; very rare. The pregnancy was over far too soon and our baby, our long awaited little boy, would not be coming home in July.

The months following our loss were incredibly difficult. It was hard to see the pain in my husband's eyes as he remained so strong for me. Our house felt empty and so did our hearts. I ended up requiring a second procedure eight weeks later because there was tissue left behind, and felt like I started the grieving process all over again. I would not wish this pain on anyone. Nobody deserves to experience such intense sadness. Nobody.

Now we must move forward. Once my body has healed and the doctor gives the green light, we will begin to prepare for our first frozen embryo transfer. We only have two embryos left, and are praying that those are our babies waiting to come home with us. All we can do is hope and pray that our dream of becoming parents will soon be realized. That's all we can do, and we will never give up. We were meant to be parents, and now we have a special little angel watching over us in heaven.

Sandy's Story

*Sandy actually has a couple of blogs, all focused on fertility over the age of 40. She has given me permission to use her story from her website, which you can find the link to at the back of this book. Please also check out her book, <u>You Can Get Pregnant Over 40, Naturally II</u>. Details on where to buy are in the back of this book as well as on her blog.

I didn't want kids when I was younger. I grew up in the "baby boomer" era when it was somewhat "uncool" to be a wife and mother. I was somewhat caught up in the feminist movement and my goal was to become a woman in business. I also grew up with a bad impression of marriage and family. My parents were quite mismatched and they didn't have the time or energy to put into their kids. As a result, getting married and having kids was very low on my priority list. I finally got married when I was 36 and I realized that having a child could be a very rewarding experience. We started trying to get pregnant about a year after we got married.

After a year, I got a referral to a reproductive endocrinologist. We tried fertility drugs, seven cycles of inseminations, and IVF twice. My first IVF resulted in a twin pregnancy, however, one was in my fallopian tube. I had to undergo surgery to remove my fallopian tube, and the other pregnancy died in my uterus. My second IVF also resulted in an ectopic pregnancy in my other tube, but I was given a drug to treat the ectopic pregnancy, which preserved my one remaining tube. At this point we decided enough was enough and it was time to stop undergoing fertility treatments.

We almost gave up on being parents. However, at this point it seemed that no matter where I went, or who I talked to, I would hear about yet another woman over the age of 40 who conceived naturally. I had the overwhelming feeling like I could get pregnant if I did the right things. I still had one fallopian tube and I decided to embark on my all-natural journey to pregnancy. I quit a high stress job, I researched foods which promote fertility, I confronted my less-than-perfect upbringing, I started a program of meditation and visualization, and I found myself pregnant naturally just months after completing fertility treatments.

To make a long story short, I got pregnant naturally three times in my 40s even with one fallopian tube. All of these pregnancies ended in miscarriage. However, I felt that each time I got pregnant, I was closer to my goal. I got pregnant again right before my 44th birthday and had a completely normal pregnancy and normal delivery, which resulted in the birth of my daughter.

Wendy's Story

My husband and I got married the summer of 1999. He is five years older and was in his late 20s when we got married. We didn't want to wait too long before trying to have a baby, but we also wanted to enjoy some time with just the two of us. We decided to wait about a year before trying to have a baby.

I was on birth control before we got married because of irregular cycles. I continued on birth control until a few months before we wanted to try to have a baby. We were super excited when we thought it was the "right time" to have a baby. Little did I know how difficult and emotional this journey would be. Because the birth control regulated my cycles, you can imagine what happened when I went off. My cycles were once again very irregular. Needless to say, it made it hard to predict good timing to have intercourse.

After 12 months of heartache and negative pregnancy tests, we decided to seek the help of a fertility specialist. By the time we sought help, I was run down emotionally. I always wanted to be a mom and I was losing hope that it would ever happen. It was hard on our marriage, too. All I could focus on was how much I wanted a baby. I was getting more and more depressed and my husband didn't really understand, even though our journey was hard on him, too. It made our physical relationship stressed, and sex was never spontaneous anymore.

Once seeking help with a specialist, we went through a battery of testing. It was determined that my husband had borderline low sperm count and that our infertility was most likely due to my irregular cycles. The doctor put me on a low dose of Clomid along with a drug to start my cycle and another one to stimulate egg growth. Still nothing was working. I was taking time off my full-time job to travel 30 to 40 minutes each way, and it was hard to explain to my coworkers. It was difficult hearing pregnancy announcements and unwanted advice on how to become pregnant.

After several months on the lower dose of Clomid, the doctors kept putting me on higher and higher doses until I was at the highest dose possible. The clinic was starting to prep me to begin with shots the following month. This next step was even more difficult to swallow, because up until this point, the financial part hadn't been too bad. I had good insurance, but my insurance company would not cover any of the shots. Even though we knew it was worth the cost, it was hard knowing we would have a hard time making ends meet. I started to research which pharmacies would be the cheapest to purchase the shots. I spent quite a bit of time calling one pharmacy after the next.

While we were still researching, we tried one more round of the highest dose of Clomid. The next month I missed my period, but didn't think much of it because of my irregular cycles, and honestly didn't think I could handle another negative pregnancy test. Just before we were ready to set up an appointment to start the shots, I got a call from the clinic that my blood work showed I was pregnant! The last round of Clomid had worked and I was finally expecting our first child.

We of course were ecstatic and in a state of shock. We had been on this journey for about 18 months now and it was hard to believe it was over. My pregnancy went well up until my 36th week when my water broke out of the blue. Our son was born one month early and spent a week in the neonatal unit, but now he is a perfectly healthy 15-year-old.

We went on to adopt a son and had two biological daughters without the help of a specialist. The infertility journey was hard and long, but it opened my eyes and made each and every one of our kids that much more special. It has also helped me to be more sensitive to those who may be going through the heartache of infertility and wanting a baby so bad it hurts. I know not to ask seemingly harmless questions or to give advice such as, "When are you going to have kids?" and," Why don't you try this?" Although I would rather not have had to experience infertility, it has made me that much more grateful for my children God has blessed me with.

Zoey's Story

Two. It's just a number. But it means so much more to me. Two is a couple, not a family. "Just two?" is often what we are asked in a restaurant or when renting or buying a house. "Why do you want so much space just for two people?" Should we go live in a box instead? Do we not have the same rights as everyone else for space, for a garden? Two, I guess is an inferior number. That's been my experience anyway.

I have problems with other numbers, too. Less than 5% were the chances I was told I would be successful getting pregnant without medical intervention. 10 years trying to have a baby that never came. 20 years chasing an education and career (as I was assured there was plenty of time for marriage and children later). 30s, the age I started trying. 40s, the age of major medical problems that threatened my life and made me realize I could be okay without children as long as I had my health back. 50, the age I am now and finally realizing it's just going to be the two of us, and that's okay.

We thought about fostering. We thought about adoption. But both have their pitfalls, and we have recently realized, after much praying for direction, neither is right for us.

Some ladies in similar life situations have asked me if it gets easier. Yes, and, well, no. Yes, only because it just becomes your accepted reality. Once you get older (relatively speaking) and are passed the "it could still happen" age, the hope of children is replaced by other things: traveling, creative endeavors, and planning for retirement, instead of saving for college, weddings, and grandchildren. At least the extra financial security is nice.

And no. For as much as I can put the dream of children away, their absence still sneaks up on me. On holidays: Thanksgiving with the table set for just two; Christmas with no bikes to put together at the 11th hour and no "toy of the year" we just have to get; Mother's Day, ugh! That used to be my hide out day, my "avoid church" Sunday. Now it's my spa day, a day to watch movies in my PJs, or soak in a tub for hours. I still find the commercials on TV and in the newspaper annoying. They don't make nearly the fuss about Father's Day. I wonder if anyone knows that Mother's Day was actually started for women who had lost sons in the war? Now it's become a slap in the face to women who have lost babies or never could have children.

But more than these obvious holidays, the childless sadness finds me, not on any special day, but on a "random any day". Maybe I'm sitting in a restaurant and it's suddenly besieged by babies, strollers, children under two. Recently we've taken to sitting in the bar section in restaurants to avoid this. Some people might say, "You must not like kids!" Not true. I was a kid once myself, and I was downright cute, too. But maybe I like them too much, and sitting in the glaring spotlight of reality is just too much to bear sometimes. The light is much better in the bar seating. There's no whining, and they have big screen TVs, too.

Reality also gets me when I come across a long-forgotten pregnancy test tucked away in a drawer, a book about a special fertility diet lying in wait under a pile of cookbooks, or computer bookmarks for that perfect crib or christening gown. I've tried to purge these things over the years, but there are still hidden landmines around, and they will get me despite my best efforts.

There are good things I have admit to just being the two of us. We enjoy sleeping in on the weekends and napping in the afternoon. We stay up late, binge watching TV shows and watching whatever we want, at whatever time, and don't worry about impressionable minds or ears. We enjoy going out to lunch and dinner, shopping and traveling at a moment's notice without having to check sport and school schedules and packing a car full of strollers, car seats, baby bottles, baby food, kid's games, diaper bags, and extra clothes. We enjoy fixing fancy meals when we feel ambitious, and not preparing a meal when we're just too tired to cook, are too busy playing, traveling, or working to eat.

I never got stretchmarks, sagging skin, stubborn post-pregnancy weight and had to "get my figure back" (well, not from childbirth. Holidays are another story). At 50, I don't worry about looking good in lingerie or swimwear (so that is a bonus). Housework, sometimes I let it slide, but I don't have to worry about Junior getting into things that don't get put away immediately, like a 25-pound bag of rice or jumbo packs of toilet paper. Laundry, well, laundry is still laundry no matter the amount. I keep washing it and it keeps coming back.

We don't have a jammed-packed schedule of sports, music lessons, PTA meetings, scout meetings, bake sales, sleep overs, and summer camp that could leave us worn out, grousing about where all our time goes, with only enough energy to collapse into bed and start again the next day.

Those are some of the good things. But with good comes a cold reality: there aren't any sport events, music lessons, PTA meetings, scout meetings, bake sales, sleep overs, summer camp, first birthdays, first days of school, first dates, graduations, college plans, or dreams to share. No excitement, no goals to reach for, no setbacks and then triumphs. Sigh.

Everyday chores can bring about daydreams. When I'm cooking, I think about teaching a little one about the "magic" of making cookies: put all these ingredients in a bowl, mix them together, put it in the magic hot box, and "presto", cookies!! When washing dishes, I think about the simple beauty of blowing soap bubbles and watching them drift off into air. A child would be so amazed. Out in the garden I imagine how I could share the magic of putting a seed in the ground, waiting, and then watching a large plant come to life, produce more seeds, and start the cycle all over again.

I wonder at the complexity of our bodies. I'll never understand why some people are fertile myrtles and can get pregnant every time the wind blows up their skirt, (despite their poor health, poor life habits), while others do every type of gymnastic move and dance gyration, load up with proper nutrition, and top medical care, yet month after month, year after year nothing happens. I'll never understand it, but don't get me started on the list of things I don't understand. "Life, who knew?" That about covers it.

That's about the good and bad of it. You knew it had to be both, right? Any one that tells you it's just one or the other isn't being honest with themselves or you. I think they call that denial. I've been there.

This is all very much like the grieving process. Are you familiar with the five stages of grieving: denial, anger, bargaining, depression, and acceptance? I think I finally got to the end of it, acceptance. But are we ever really done? I spent a lot of time in stage two, anger. Sometimes I go back for a visit. (When I see someone mistreating their child, or paying more attention to their cell phone than what their kid is doing, yeah, that's anger).

Most of the time I'm in acceptance, though. I think they should have added a sixth step, avoidance/acknowledgement. That's where you learn the triggers that send you back to the other stages. Remember the bar seating? Yeah, that's acknowledgement. Not going to church on Mother's Day, skipping baby showers, that's acknowledgment.

So, we've moved on to the next phase of our lives together. This has been a hard process, not unlike life itself. We are all works in progress, until God calls us home. I'm not sure what is going to happen in our future. But unless God tells us otherwise, we will embrace the number two, be thankful for each other, our extended family, and everything else God has generously given us.

Not Alone

All of these above stories indicate you are not suffering alone, and there is something profound in knowing that! Obviously, you are not wanting other people to struggle. But it is nice knowing you're not alone in the battle.

My goal for you is that, having read these stories, you will find hope. I desire for you to feel a sense of normalcy and understanding. And my wish is that you definitely found validation for all of your feelings, decisions, emotions, actions, and experiences relating to your infertility journey.

As we close out this section of the book, there's one more thing we all need to remember. It's closely related to this one; however, the biggest difference is tangible connection.

19

We're All in This Together

The fifth and final thing that we should all remember when it comes to our own infertility journey is that there is a lot of support out there. Knowing that we're not alone is one thing. Knowing you can get connected with others in the same shoes as you is a whole other level. Believe it or not, you can receive support from people locally and as far reached as around the world.

The Buddy System

I know that I've mentioned this a couple of times before, but it bears repeating. Infertility is like a club. It's not one that you've ever wanted to join in the first place, but it's also one that you will never leave. What I mean by that is that you will never forget the journey that you are on right now. You will also probably make lasting relationships that will go on even after your infertility journey has ended. The infertility club can be a close-knit group. We're all here for one another, and we're all cheering each other on. Having a buddy that actually gets what we're experiencing makes going through infertility slightly easier.

As an example, when I first started trying to conceive, the first place I started looking for support was online. I'm the kind of person that doesn't get out much, which is the way I like it. At the time, I also didn't know a lot of people in my social circle that were going through the same things I was. So, it just made sense for me to look online for support. I came across an online forum called Two Week Wait, which I'll share more on in just a moment. As I got more and more connected, there was a group of the same specific ladies that seemed to stick together, including myself. One by one, most of us started to have children. The whole time, though, as bittersweet as moments may have been, we have all rooted each other on. None of us are on Two Week Wait any longer, but we decided to remain friends through a private Facebook group. I know that my case is not the only one out there!

So where can you find a support system? A buddy, if you will? Let's take a moment to examine all of the possibilities.

· **Locally (for those who like to physically see their support)** –

   o **Therapists.** Seeing as infertility is more than just a physical disease, but a deeply emotional one as well, some of you may benefit from getting professional help. There are licensed therapists that specialize in those who are going through infertility. These professionals know best how to get you to process through and cope with your emotions and experiences. This may not be the best example of an infertility buddy because they may not 100% understand exactly everything you're dealing with per se, but they can still offer excellent techniques, tips, advice, and support of varying degrees. This is definitely the preferred method of getting the support you need should you be in a place where you're contemplating divorce, anything illegal, and/or suicide.

   o **Infertility Centers.** Many infertility centers not only provide the treatments necessary to obtain a pregnancy, but also provide support in one way or another for those going through the treatments. They understand that infertility is difficult and there are many emotions that come with it. Whether they provide their own personal counselor, a list of local groups to get connected with, or both, they can be a useful place to check out for any support you may need.

   o **Churches.** Don't let that one word scare you. I know not everyone is comfortable with churches, but just because a support group is part of a church, it doesn't mean they're going to try to push God on you or anything. Most infertility support groups are there to support you through infertility, not to get you to become a Christian or condemn you for not being one, etc. Some of these groups may do a Bible study of some sort, but not all.

   Back in 2012, I helped create an infertility support group at my church. Though we meet at the church, we don't do any Bible studies or anything Christian related. Our main purpose is to be there for other women who are going through infertility. And,

yes, we do get women that don't go to church! I personally
believe that a church, of all places, is a safe place to go to get
the help you need. It's a place you can get some face-to-face
connection with others in the same boat as you, without any
judgement.

· International (for those who like a little bit of anonymity) –

    o **Blogs.** If you research infertility blogs, you'll quickly learn that
there are a lot of them out there. Not all of them may be
current, however, because it seems like so many women stop
once their own journey is done. Regardless of that, though,
they are great resources to follow for tips, advice, and
examples of how to cope. Some women get very candid with
their journey and willingly share it for the whole world to see.
Seeing their posts can help us feel like we really know the
person even though there's technically no real connection
made. Other than commenting on posts the writer may make,
the type of support here is more one-sided. That doesn't mean
it's less important, though! Blogs have helped many women
navigate their own journey.

    o **Online Forums.** For those who like actual conversations with
others going through the same struggle as you are, try looking
into online forums. There are many of them out there, and I'll
list some of them in just a moment. But these boards connect
people that have something in common besides infertility. For
example, there might be a topic on trying to conceive after
miscarriage. If you joined that group, you know that every
member there has had a miscarriage and are now trying to
conceive again. There are too many types of groups to mention
so it'd be best to just check them out for yourself. No one has
to know the real you if you're worried about that sort of thing.
However, I think you'll quickly feel comfortable enough to
share who you are, and lasting friendships will be made. To get
involved now, just go to one of these websites and find their
forums. You can also just research trying to conceive boards
for other options.

§ **Two Week Wait** (www.twoweekwait.com). This is the forum that I got involved with. It's easy to navigate and everyone is super friendly. They have a lot of different topics you can become a part of as well.

§ **RESOLVE** (www.resolve.org). Not only does RESOLVE had all kinds of information on infertility itself, they also offer support groups. They are absolutely a well-trusted place to check out for help.

§ **JustMommies** (www.justmommies.com). JustMommies is a website that claims to be the friendliest place for moms and moms-to-be. However, they are also one of the friendliest places to go for those trying to become moms-to-be. Their forums have many options you can get familiar with that have to deal with infertility.

o **Facebook Groups.** I think this is one of the most real-time, anytime type of support you can get. Most of us are already on Facebook for various reasons so why not join an infertility group as well? There are quite a few of them out there, and they're easy to join. The women (and men if the group is co-ed) are super friendly and extremely helpful. The examples below are just a couple of the ones that I would recommend joining. To do so, just type the names of these groups in the search bar while in Facebook. Go to the group's page and then click 'Join'.

§ Seeking God Through Infertility and Child Loss

§ Infertility Support – Christians

§ Christian Infertility Support Group

§ Infertility Issues, Awareness and Support Group

§ Infertility, Pregnancy Difficulty, and Miscarriage Support Group

Reach Out

While I hope that many parts of this book have been helpful to you, I do understand that not all help can come just by reading a book. That is why it's super important to figure out what our needs are and then to not be afraid to reach out to others for that support. Help is out there and very much available. All we need to do is find it.

Before we move on to the next section of the book, I want to leave you with a quote by Dave G. Llewellyn. For those who may not know who he is, he's the administrator of the Facebook page, Inspire Me, a place to be inspired and to inspire others. This quote was something I saw on one of Dave's memes. On the meme were two kittens, one looking like it was planting a big kiss on the other's forehead. It was very cute, but of course I love cats so may be a little biased to that opinion. Anyway, the quote said, "Just being there for someone can sometimes bring hope when all seems hopeless."

I felt like that was fitting to this chapter because as we seek out support from others, they can truly brighten things up for us and give us a new hope. This sense of connection can be refreshing. After all, there's someone you can turn to. Someone to talk to. Someone who'll listen. There's no judgement. No condemnation. No guilt trips or manipulation. There's helpful advice, tips, understanding, and unconditional support.

The list of benefits one gets from getting connected could go on and on and on. I'm so thankful there are many ways to do so. I want to encourage you to find a buddy or buddies if you haven't already done so. I know that you won't regret it.

Part Six

***

What to Cling to Through the Journey

20

You're My Inspiration

As one who has gone through infertility, I know there were a couple of things I needed to cling to in order to carry me through the journey, seeing as I didn't know how it would end or even when it would. The same is true for you. In this chapter, we'll look at the first thing we all need to cling to, and that is inspiration.

Everyone finds inspiration in different places so it's a good thing there is a lot of it out there. For some of you, it may be in your faith. Things like Bible verses, prayer, and spending time in church-related activities really encourage you. Others of you may find that books such as this, music, movies, or even famous quotes seem to move you. Some of you may even get inspired just by building relationships with other women who are in the same shoes as you. Like I said, there's a lot of options out there to give you hope and encouragement.

Wherever you find your inspiration that enables you to keep on trucking through your infertility journey, cling to it. Cling to whatever hope you find because not only do you need it, but because a little bit can go a long way, and there are bound to be moments where you'll need to pull that inspiration out so that you can make it through.

A Little Bit of This, A Little Bit of That

If you don't mind, in the space below I want to share some things that might help you remain hopeful. I'm including a little bit of quotes, books, music, and Bible verses, as well as one movie, so that there's a little something for everyone. Some of these suggestions are things that either helped me as I went through infertility or that inspire me today. Other suggestions are from what other women found/find helpful. You can also find more by researching various things on the Internet. As a side note, if applicable, I have provided links in the back of the book should there be something you want to look into.

· **Quotes (for those who find inspiration in the spoken word) –**

o "Let the Lord do as He wills to us! He will never be unkind to us! He has always been our friend – He will never be our foe! He will never put us into the furnace – unless He means to purge the dross out of us. Nor will there be one degree more heat in that furnace than is absolutely necessary – there will always be mercy to balance the misery – and strength supplied to support the burden to be borne. Oh, children of God, your Father knows best! Leave everything in His hands and be at peace – for all is well." – Charles Spurgeon

o "The longer you wait for something, the more you'll appreciate it when you get it. Because anything worth having is definitely worth waiting for." – Anonymous

o "When the world says, 'Give up,' hope whispers, 'Try one more time.'" – Anonymous

o "Sometimes in tragedy we find out life's purpose. The eye sheds a tear to find its focus." – Robert Brault

o "Fall seven times, get up eight." – Japanese Proverb

o "Don't be discouraged. It's often the last key in the bunch that opens the lock." – Anonymous

o "It's going to be okay in the end. If it's not okay, it's not the end." – Anonymous

o "Change your thoughts and you change your world." – Norman Vincent Peale

o "Courage is going from failure to failure without ever losing enthusiasm." – Winston Churchill

o "Even the darkest night will end and the sun will rise." – Victor Hugo

o "You may not control all the events that happen to you, but you can decide not to be reduced by them." – Maya Angelou

o "What isn't today, might be tomorrow." – Anonymous

o "I am not afraid of storms, for I am learning how to sail my ship." – Louisa May Alcott

o "There's no telling how many miles you have to run while chasing a dream." – Anonymous

o "When nothing is sure, everything is possible." – Margaret Drabble

o "I can't change the direction of the wind, but I can adjust my sails to always reach my destination." – Jimmy Dean

o "Believe you can and you're halfway there." – Theodore Roosevelt

o "We must let go of the life we have planned, so as to accept the one waiting for us." – Joseph Campbell

o "Nothing is impossible, the word itself says, 'I'm possible.'" – Audrey Hepburn

o "Start by doing what's necessary; then do what's possible; and suddenly you are doing the impossible." – Francis of Assisi

o "Keep your face always toward the sunshine - and shadows will fall behind you." – Walt Whitman

o "What lies behind you and what lies in front of you, pales in comparison to what lies inside of you." – Ralph Waldo Emerson

· **Books (for those who find inspiration in the written word) –**

o Hannah's Hope: Seeking God's Heart in the Midst of Infertility, Miscarriage, and Adoption Loss by Jennifer Saake

§ This book is perfect for both those who are going through infertility as well as for those who want to support others going through it. The author not only uses her own story, but weaves it together with the story of the biblical character, Hannah.

o <u>Not Alone: A Literary and Spiritual Companion for Those Confronted with Infertility & Miscarriage</u> edited by Jessica Snell

    § This book features stories from other women who have gone through infertility and miscarriage.

o <u>Plus or Minus: Keeping Your Life, Faith, and Love Together Through Infertility</u> by Matt and Cheri Appling

    § This very relatable book shares how couples survived their infertility journey.

o <u>Empty Womb, Aching Heart: Hope and Help for Those Struggling with Infertility</u> by Marlo Schalesky

    § This book shares honest, open stories from couples who have gone through infertility.

· **Music (for those who find inspiration in song)** –

o "<u>Praise You in This Storm</u>" by <u>Casting Crowns</u>

    § This song came out in 2005, but I never got to really loving it until after my miscarriage in 2007. The whole song is fantastic, but here are the lyrics that really resonated with me:

        · "And every tear I've cried, you hold in your hand. You never left my side. And though my heart is torn, I will praise You in this storm."

o "<u>I am God</u>" by <u>Kirk Franklin</u> featuring <u>Toby Mac</u>

    § The chorus of this song is actually my mantra. Anytime I get worried or have any doubt about anything, these are the words I remember:

        · "Be still and know I am God."

o "<u>It Is Well</u>" by <u>Bethel Music</u>

§ This is a newer song, but is a different spin on an old classic hymn. Anything by Bethel is moving in one way or another. What speaks to me from "It Is Well" is this:

- · "Far be it from me to not believe, even when my eyes can't see. And this mountain that's in front of me will be thrown into the midst of the sea. Through it all, through it all, my eyes are on You. Through it all, through it all, it is well. Through it all, through it all, my eyes are on You. And it is well, it is well. So, let go my soul and trust in Him. The waves and wind still know His name. It is well with my soul."

o "I Would Die for That" by Kellie Coffey

§ This whole song is about infertility. It's no wonder this tends to be one of the top songs infertility sufferers go to for inspiration. Look at these lyrics and try not to cry:

- · "All I want is a family like everyone else I see. And I won't understand it if it's not meant to be. 'Cause I would die for that. Just to have one chance to hold in my hands all that they have. I would die for that."

- · "Sometimes it's hard to conceive, with all that I've got, and all I've achieved. What I want most before my time is gone is to hear the words, "I love you, Mom.""

o "Light Up the Sky" by The Afters

§ This song came out the same year my first son was born. I love the assurance of God's love, and the fact that we are never alone. If you get a chance, watch the music video to this song. It's powerful! Here is part of why this song inspires me:

- · "When stars are hiding the clouds, I don't feel them shining. When I can't see beyond my doubt, the silver lining. When I've almost reached the end, like a flood you're rushing in. Your love is rushing in."

o "Strong Enough" by Matthew West

§ I think that this song is a great reminder that we aren't strong enough on our own, even though we think we are. We can do everything through Christ, though! Check out just a small part of this song:

- · "'Cause I'm broken down to nothing, but I'm still holding on to the one thing: You are God and You are strong when I am weak. I can do all things through Christ who gives me strength. And I don't have to be, I don't have to be strong enough."

o "Song of Hope" by Robbie Seay Band

§ The title alone on this upbeat song gives it all away. It's all about singing a song of hope. I love the chorus:

- · "I will sing a song of hope, sing along. God of heaven, come down. Heaven come down. Just to know You are near is enough. God of heaven, come down. Heaven come down."

o "So Hard" by Dixie Chicks

§ Two of the members of Dixie Chicks went through infertility so they sing this song with a lot of heart. Look at this verse from this song:

- · "It felt like a given, something a woman's born to do. A natural ambition, to see a reflection of me and you. And I'd feel so guilty if that was a gift

I couldn't give. And could you be happy if life wasn't how we pictured it?"

o "Anyway" by Martina McBride

§ This song debuted in 2007 and really inspired me to keep on trying. We are to keep on going no matter what the outcome is. This one part of the song really hit home with me:

· "God is great, but sometimes life ain't good. And when I pray, it doesn't always turn out like I think it should. But I do it anyway. I do it anyway."

o "Need You Now" by Plumb

§ You know a song is going to be good if right off the bat the lyrics speak to you. I felt this way with "Need You Now." There are moments I still cling to the words here:

· "Well, everybody's got a story to tell. And everybody's got a wound to be healed. I want to believe there's beauty here. 'Cause oh, I get so tired of holding on. I can't let go, I can't move on. I want to believe there's meaning here. How many times have you heard me cry out, "God, please take this?" How many times have you given me strength to just keep breathing? Oh, I need you. God, I need you now."

o "The Climb" by Miley Cyrus

§ This song is ultra-motivating. No matter what is going on, we have to keep going, keep trying. After all, it's not about what we're going through. It's all about the process in which to conquer it. Take a look at this part of the song:

· "There's always going to be another mountain.
I'm always gonna wanna make it move. Always
gonna be an uphill battle. Sometimes I'm gonna
have to lose. Ain't about how fast I get there.
Ain't about what's waiting on the other side. It's
the climb."

· **Bible Verses (for those who find inspiration within their faith) –**

o "Lord, you know the hopes of the helpless. Surely you will hear
their cries and comfort them." – Psalm 10:17

o "The Lord is close to the brokenhearted; He rescues those whose
spirits are crushed." – Psalm 34:18

o "Be still and know that I am God! I will be honored by every
nation. I will be honored throughout the world." – Psalm 46:10

o "He gives the childless woman a family, making her a happy
mother. Praise the Lord!" – Psalm 113:9

o "Children are a gift from the Lord; they are a reward from Him.
Children born to a young man are like arrows in a warrior's
hands. How joyful is the man whose quiver is full of them! He
will not be put to shame when he confronts his accusers at the
city gates." – Psalm 127: 3-5

o "Trust in the Lord with all your heart; do not depend on your
own understanding. Seek His will in all you do, and He will
show you which path to take." – Proverbs 3:5-6

o "But those who trust in the Lord will find new strength. They
will soar high on wings like eagles. They will run and not grow
weary. They will walk and not faint." – Isaiah 40:31

o "When you go through deep waters, I will be with you. When
you go through rivers of difficulty, you will not drown. When
you walk through the fire of oppression, you will not be
burned up; the flames will not consume you." – Isaiah 43:2

o ""For I know the plans I have for you," says the Lord. "They are plans for good and not for disaster, to give you a future and a hope."" – Jeremiah 29:11

o "Then Jesus said, "Come to me, all of you who are weary and carry heavy burdens, and I will give you rest. Take my yoke upon you. Let me teach you, because I am humble and gentle at heart, and you will find rest for your souls."" – Matthew 11:28-29

o "I tell you, you can pray for anything, and if you believe that you've received it, it will be yours." – Mark 11:24

o "Because of our faith, Christ has brought us into this place of undeserved privilege where we now stand, and we confidently and joyfully look forward to sharing God's glory. We can rejoice, too, when we run into problems and trials, for we know that they help us develop endurance. And endurance develops strength of character, and character strengthens our confident hope of salvation. And this hope will not lead to disappointment. For we know how dearly God loves us, because He has given us the Holy Spirit to fill our hearts with his love." – Romans 5:2-5

o "And we know that God causes everything to work together for the good of those who love God and are called according to his purpose for them." – Romans 8:28

o "That is why we never give up. Though our bodies are dying, our spirits are being renewed every day. For our present troubles are small and won't last very long. Yet they produce for us a glory that vastly outweighs them and will last forever! So, we don't look at the troubles we can see now; rather, we fix our gaze on things that cannot be seen. For the things we see now will soon be gone, but the things we cannot see will last forever." – 2 Corinthians 4:16-18

o "Don't worry about anything; instead, pray about everything. Tell God what you need, and thank Him for all He has done.

Then you will experience God's peace, which exceeds anything we can understand. His peace will guard your hearts and minds as you live in Christ Jesus." – Philippians 4:6-7

o "For I can do everything through Christ, who gives me strength." – Philippians 4:13

o "And we are confident that He hears us whenever we ask for anything that pleases Him." – 1 John 5:14

o "He will wipe every tear from their eyes, and there will be no more death or sorrow or crying or pain. All these things are gone forever." – Revelation 21:4

· **Movie (for those who find inspiration in what they watch)** –

o <u>Facing the Giants</u>

§ This movie was made in 2006, and each and every time I watch it, I tear up. It is a Christian film so I would understand if there were some of you who wouldn't want to give it a try, but I really hope you will consider it. The premise of the movie is that everything is going wrong for this one man, including the fact he just found out he is the reason he and his wife aren't getting pregnant. Using his faith, he faces the giants of fear and failure head on until ultimately winning his battles. I say it again, it is a phenomenal movie that I highly recommend.

As you can see, there is a wide variety of options to choose from to find your inspiration. Let me tell you something, though. It was hard picking and choosing which things to include in this book because there are many more possibilities. Especially when it came to music. Music is something I really connect with, and so many songs move me in different ways. Hopefully I've made some good choices by including various genres. And as I said before, if you are interested in maybe watching a music video of one of the songs, or perhaps buying a book, or finding any information out about any of the above examples, I have many links listed at the back of the book for your convenience.

Seeing that everyone is different, however, none of these may even do a thing for you because you connect with other things. That's okay! I won't feel offended if nothing helped you. The main thing is you know what inspires you. Looking back, what would you add to this list?

A 31-Day Exercise

While doing some research, I found a website that proved to be helpful. The website is AmateurNester.com, and is run by Lisa Newton, an amazing woman who went through infertility herself. AmateurNester's purpose is to encourage and inspire others during their infertility journey, and they do so by providing many resources, including interviews with many others who know the infertility struggle. After becoming familiar with the whole site, I not only wished it was around when I was going through infertility, but I found that the site does live up to its specific purpose.

I mention all of that because of an exercise that Lisa Newton created that I happened to stumble across through Facebook. It's something that is great for those that pray. If you are one who doesn't pray, you might still find this interesting and useful. There's never a bad time to start praying! However, if you wish, you can still pass through this section and make your way to the end of the chapter should you not be interested in anything to do with prayer.

Anyway, Lisa Newton's exercise is to pray your way through infertility by praying for something specific each day for 31 days. As a bonus, there is a scripture reading you can meditate on as well. The exercise is listed here, but if you head over to her website, you'll be able to get a beautiful printable of this very thing. Please also be sure to check out her website as well for her books (she's got one on prayer and scripture) that correspond to this!

· **Day 1.** Pray for clarity – Isaiah 30:21

· **Day 2.** Pray for comfort – Isaiah 51:3

· **Day 3.** Pray for community – Galatians 6:2

· **Day 4.** Pray for confidence – Jeremiah 17:7

· **Day 5.** Pray for contentment – 1 Timothy 6:8

· **Day 6.** Pray for courage – Psalm 31:24

· **Day 7.** Pray for discernment – 1 John 4:1

· **Day 8.** Pray for endurance – Colossians 1:11

· **Day 9.** Pray for faith – Luke 17:5

· **Day 10.** Pray for freedom from fear – Psalm 34:4

· **Day 11.** Pray for freedom from jealousy & envy – Job 5:2

· **Day 12.** Pray for your future family – Isaiah 44:3

· **Day 13.** Pray for God's glory – Matthew 5:16

· **Day 14.** Pray for grace – Ephesians 6:24

· **Day 15.** Pray for gratefulness – 1 Thessalonians 5:16-18

· **Day 16.** Pray for hope – Psalm 62:5

· **Day 17.** Pray for integrity – Proverbs 20:7

· **Day 18.** Pray for joy – Nehemiah 8:10

· **Day 19.** Pray for mercy – Psalm 28:2

· **Day 20.** Pray for obedience – Psalm 51:12

· **Day 21.** Pray for others – James 5:16

· **Day 22.** Pray for patience – Habakkuk 2:3

· **Day 23.** Pray for peace – Philippians 4:7

· **Day 24.** Pray for strength – Psalm 73:27

· **Day 25.** Pray for sufficient finances – Philippians 4:19

· **Day 26.** Pray for true belief in God's promises – Romans 8:28

· **Day 27.** Pray for trust – Psalm 37:5

· **Day 28.** Pray for wisdom – Proverbs 2:3

· **Day 29.** Pray for wise decisions – Proverbs 19:2

· **Day 30.** Pray for your marriage – Colossians 3:14

· **Day 31.** Pray for your specific situation –
  Colossians 4:2

Always Hope

No matter how dire your situation is, and trust me, I know that there will be many times in your journey where you'll feel as if you can't go on, please know that there is always hope. It may not seem like it and it may be hard to find, but hope is always there. It is my goal that something from this book, including the stories you've read earlier from other women, and many of the items listed above, will renew your spirit and give you hope everlasting. Just remember to take one day at a time, one breath at a time, and cling to whatever it is that inspires you. For that brings hope!

Let's now shift to a second thing we need to cling to throughout our journey.

This Too Shall Pass

Clinging to whatever inspires you through your infertility journey is extremely important, but just as equally so is clinging to the truth of what infertility really is. I'm not talking about its definition or what it represents. The truth I'm referring to here is two-fold, and contrary to how you may feel or how your situation may be panning out at the moment, these two truths remain constant. Let's check out what these two truths are.

The End

Okay. This may not be the end of the book, but you'll soon see why that heading is fitting here. Did you know that your journey is only for a season? Of course, I'm not talking about spring, summer, fall, or winter. I'm talking about the fact it's only for just a part of your life. I know there are moments where, in the deepest, darkest parts of your infertility journey, you feel like you can't go on and that this pain will never go away. You think to yourself there's no end to this tunnel. But I've got great news!

Infertility may be a disease, and it is definitely a disease that sucks. However, it's also a type of disease that always comes to an end! This is not a lifelong debilitating disease. The effects, memories, and relationships may be, unfortunately, but the disease itself is not. There is an end, and once you reach your end, you'll have a beautifully written story you can call your own that you may end up choosing to share with others.

What might the end look like for you? It's different for everyone, but the truth still remains: infertility will be conquered one way or another. There will be an end for each and every one of you!

You might:

· **Get pregnant!** In today's day and age, with medical technology rapidly advancing, this is an outcome that is getting more and more realistic. I certainly hope that this is true for you, but there are other great possibilities as well.

· **Adopt!** Some people just have their hearts inclined towards adopting. There is a huge need out there, and I can't think of no better people to adopt than those who actually want children.

· **Use a surrogate!** This method of having a child may not be the most popular, and I know there are a lot of legal issues surrounding it, but surrogacy does happen quite often. If this is the only way you and your partner can have a biological child, why not?

· **Keep trying!** Okay. Bear with me here a minute. You might think that if you are still trying then your infertility journey hasn't come to an end. I'd beg to differ. There is a difference between being in the midst of your journey, desperately aching for a child to call your own in such a way that you can't stand waiting, and coming to a peaceful decision that while you still try, that ache will no longer control you. Basically, you're at a point in your journey where, yes, you'd still like a child, but if it never happened, you are okay with it. If that is where you are, I say you have come to the end of your journey.

· **Remain a family of two!** There is nothing wrong with deciding that having children is just not in the cards for you. There may actually be some pluses to not having children, and so some couples go this route. They choose to use their money on luxuries instead.

There are other options out there as well, but no matter where your journey takes you, any and all of these outcomes are okay. No outcome is better than another. Just because one couple gets pregnant, it doesn't make them any more of a conqueror than the couple who adopts, or the one who decides to just stay a family of two. As long as you have reached a place where you are at peace with the decision you've made regarding your infertility, you have reached the end.

Before moving on to the second truth of infertility that we all need to cling to, I want to leave you with this quote that was also shared in the last chapter. It's so spot-on that it bears repeating. An anonymous person once said, "It's going to be okay in the end. If it's not okay, it's not the end." This applies here. If you aren't okay with where you are at in your journey, it's not the end. Once you're end does come, though, it'll be okay. Not okay for just your partner or okay for your parents, friends, or whoever. It'll be okay for YOU!

Who You Are

The second and last truth I will share with you in regard to infertility is that it does not define who you are. I was given permission by a member of an infertility group I'm a part of on Facebook to share what she mentioned regarding how she'd define infertility. She said that she defines infertility as just something she's going through, which means she's not stuck there. That was our first truth we looked at. She then went on to say our second truth, that infertility doesn't define her. In other words, she is more than her ability to procreate.

This is true for every single one of us! I know that it's easy to allow infertility to make us feel worthless, or unfit, or abnormal, or even less than a woman. After all, we're supposed to be able to carry on the human race, and the idea of having babies is usually planted in our minds at a very young age. Therefore, all that infertility makes us feel must be true. Not so! We are so much more than just the ability to have children or not.

There are many things out there that you could use to define yourself, including, but not limited to, what you do for a living, your passions, your relationships, your personality, the things you support, and so on and so on. For those who believe in God, I would dare say the most important way to define ourselves is by looking at who we are in Christ. To me, that's the only definition that counts.

Anyway, never, under any circumstances, allow infertility to be one of those things that define you. It doesn't so don't let it. You are so much more than whether you can have a baby or not. I hope you can realize that.

All of this information I just shared in this short chapter, the fact that infertility always has an end and the fact that infertility does not define who you are, is something we need to cling to. When we keep these truths locked away in our brains, believing them with all that we have, we will not lose to this battle of the body, heart, and mind. Clinging to these truths will keep us moving forward, with each day that passes bringing us one more day closer to the end of that dark and lonely tunnel.

Part Seven

***

A Final Word

Anything Goes

This final chapter is going to seem redundant and that is because it is. Here I will highlight some of the main things from this book and show you one major theme. You'll quickly learn that this theme is the fact that anything, and I mean anything, pretty much goes when it comes to your infertility journey.

First off, though there are many, many women out there who are going through infertility, from dawn of creation until now and from the rich to the poor, none of these women are you and none of their journeys are your journey. This means that no one will quite understand what you are going through. The only one who really knows is you. Your partner may be a close second, but he still isn't even you. So, having said that, your journey is your journey and it is unique. Own it! Let no one try to belittle your situation and/or make you and your journey less important than others.

A second thing is that all your thoughts, feelings, and emotions are all normal. You will have highs and you will have lows. There may be days you aren't happy with the way you're feeling, or you may not like the person you've become. It happens to us all, and those stages will pass at some point. Seek help if you think those emotions are truly getting the best of you, such as you're contemplating hurting yourself or others, and/or doing something illegal.

A third point that closely follows everything I just said is that how you play out your infertility journey is up to you, and that whatever you decide is okay. Please don't be pressured into doing something you're not comfortable with just because someone else did it and had success. Don't even let doctors manipulate you or try to take charge of your journey. No one should be making your decisions except for you and maybe your partner. That's it!

On top of that, a fourth point is that whatever decisions you do make, don't let others' advice or comments affect you. They don't get it and never will. Therefore, the things they say to you should hold little to no value. No one has the right to make you feel bad, like you're making poor decisions, or being foolish.

The fifth thing I want to say is that just because other people may be going through something that is deemed worse than what you are going through, that does not invalidate your struggle. A struggle is a struggle is a struggle.

Before We Part Ways

All in all, I want you to know everything in this book is meant to come alongside you and help you process your journey. I know that you may not agree with everything stated within these pages, especially when it comes to matters around faith, but please understand that a lot of these things are just my plain old opinion around what I found helpful. Many things are also ideas and tips I had gotten from other women who are or have been in your shoes. So please understand that I'm not trying to come across as insensitive or as if I'm trying to undermine you in any way. Every journey is different and they all have their easy and tough spots. Also, everyone handles things in their own unique way. That's probably the only beauty about infertility: that every case is so different and yet it's all normal, expected, and even okay.

As I close out this book and say goodbye, please remember there is always hope, and if you can come to a place where you are at peace with the situation you've been dealt with, know that you are a conqueror. My best wishes to you as you travel your journey!

Dear Reader,

First of all, thank you so much for taking a chance on me and this book. It means so much to me that you would give me the benefit of the doubt when it comes to helping you in some way along your life's journey.

Having said that, I want to express my deepest sympathies to you. Knowing that you're reading this book means that you must be going through infertility, or at the very least, know someone who is. That road is a tough one and I wouldn't wish it on anyone. I'm sorry for what life has dealt you.

I have two favors to ask of you. If you have found any information to be incorrect, misrepresented, and/or extremely insensitive, please let me know right away. That was not my intent for this book so I am more than happy to take a look at what was written and change accordingly.

The second favor I ask of you is to please take a quick moment to leave a review. Reviews help authors, especially indie authors such as myself, a lot. Your review doesn't have to be long. I just ask that it's honest.

Thank you, again, for reading this book. I hope that you have found it helpful, and that you are left feeling better about all the things you're going through. May you be inspired to get through each day, kicking infertility in the behind. I wish you the best!

Warmest regards,

Frances Hoelsema

Notes

All scripture quotations are taken from the Holy Bible, New Living Translation (NLT). I used BibleGateway, a searchable online Bible in over 150 versions and 50 languages, to aid in researching the correct verses I wanted to use. You can find their website at http://www.biblegateway.com/

While I made every effort to provide accurate Internet addresses at the time of publication, I assume no responsibility for errors, or the changes that occur after publication. Further, I assume no responsibility for third-party websites or their content.

Any persons without a personal website will be linked to their page on Wikipedia (https://www.wikipedia.org/). This way you can at least gather more information on who it is I am talking about. Hopefully from there you can expand your research should you be looking for more information.

Lyrics provided were found on MetroLyrics, who I recommend using when searching for song lyrics. The website is http://www.metrolyrics.com/

Part One: First Things First

    1. Getting Pregnant Is NOT Easy
- Pregnancy/fertility statistics were found on a website called Our Baby Namer. The direct link is http://www.ourbabynamer.com/ttc/getting-pregnant.html
- Miscarriage statistics were found on a website called Verywell. The direct link is https://www.verywell.com/making-sense-of-miscarriage-statistics-2371721
- *Life's Greatest Miracle* was a show that aired on PBS. Certain statements from the transcript were used. http://www.pbs.org/wgbh/nova/body/life-greatest-miracle.html

    2. What Infertility Really Is
- RESOLVE: The National Infertility Association is a resource that is used throughout the book. In this chapter, I listed some facts about infertility that can be found on their website. http://www.resolve.org/about/fast-facts-about-fertility.html

Part Two: What to Expect for Yourself

    3. Say What?
- I referenced Urban Dictionary. To find out more about it, check out their website at http://www.urbandictionary.com
- WebMD was used for all medical terms related to infertility. http://www.webmd.com/baby/glossary-of-fertility-terms
- RESOLVE was used for all infertility acronyms. http://www.resolve.org/support/Managing-Infertility-Stress/infertility-acronyms.html

    4. Our Bodies Are Pretty Cool – Well, Most of The Time
- WebMD was used to provide information on the female reproductive system. http://www.webmd.com/sex-relationships/guide/your-guide-female-reproductive-system
- To learn more about predicting ovulation by looking at fertility indicators, please check out Ovulation Calculator. http://www.ovulation-calculator.com/topics/predicting-

ovulation
- WebMD was used to list some possible pregnancy symptoms.
  http://www.webmd.com/baby/guide/pregnancy-am-i-pregnant
- I discussed our minds tricking us into thinking we're pregnant when we're not. This is considered pseudocyesis. WebMD was used to find out more about it.
  http://www.webmd.com/baby/false-pregnancy-pseudocyesis

5. Not All Rollercoasters Are Fun
- Dr. Elisabeth Kübler-Ross and her book, *On Death and Dying*, were briefly mentioned in regard to the grieving process. Here are a couple of websites to check out:
  o https://en.wikipedia.org/wiki/Elisabeth_K%C3%BCbler-Ross
  o https://www.amazon.com/dp/B0053GIJFO/
- In regard to the five stages of grief infertility sufferers go through, RESOLVE was referenced. They provided great information, as well as many tips to overcome it.
  http://www.resolve.org/support/Managing-Infertility-Stress/grieving-and-growing-creative-outlets-to-grieving-during-infertility.html

6. Let's Talk About Sex, Baby!
- The Bump was used to list sexual positions that people feel are the best for getting pregnant. https://www.thebump.com/a/best-sex-positions-for-getting-pregnant
- Here is a link for Scattergories, a game by Hasbro. Although this is from Hasbro's website, you can find the game on Amazon or even at your local Wal-Mart.
  https://www.hasbro.com/en-us/product/scattergories-game:1114DFCF-5056-9047-F58B-D14732108539
- I mentioned an article on Verywell that focused on spicing up your sex life when trying to become pregnant. It discussed the more aroused we are, the better. It also provides tips on improving your sex life. https://www.verywell.com/improving-your-sex-life-when-trying-to-get-pregnant-1960262

Part Three: What to Expect from Everyone Else

7. The Male Factor
- RESOLVE's website was used to list some causes of male infertility.
  http://www.resolve.org/about-infertility/medical-conditions/male-factor.html
- Georgia Reproductive Specialists' website has a page about the emotional effects of infertility on the couple. I referenced many things from it, including how each gender copes with infertility and tips on how to reconnect as a couple.
  http://www.ivf.com/emotion.html
- I briefly mentioned author, Gary Thomas, and his book, *Sacred Marriage*. Here is a link to his website where you can find out more about him and/or purchase his book. http://www.garythomas.com/

8. People Say the Darndest Things
- *Kids Say the Darndest Things* is a show from the late 1990s. You can find more information on it at https://en.wikipedia.org/wiki/Kids_Say_the_Darndest_Things
- The host of *Kids Say the Darndest Things* was Bill Cosby. Here is his official website: http://www.billcosby.com/
- The costs of adoption that I had mentioned were found on Adoption.com. A lot of other useful information regarding adoption is there as well.
  https://adoption.com/wiki/Adoption_Costs
- I referenced an article from a website called What Christians Want to Know that shares the truth behind what 1 Corinthians 10:13 is really saying.

http://www.whatchristianswanttoknow.com/does-God-promise-that-he-will-not-give-us-more-than-we-can-handle/

9. They Just Don't Get It
  · I referenced Shiva.com. For more information on what Shiva is and how to practice it, please see the following website: http://www.shiva.com/learning-center/
  · RESOLVE's website was used when giving ideas on how to properly interact with those who are suffering. http://www.resolve.org/support/for-family--friends/infertility-etiquette.html

10. Fertile Myrtle
  · I mentioned Dara and Christopher Sundberg, the couple who kept getting pregnant even though they had surgeries to prevent it from happening. You can find their unique story at http://woodtv.com/2016/05/12/against-the-odds-cedar-springs-family-keeps-growing/
  · I also mentioned the Duggar Family. You can find more information on them here: http://duggarfamily.com/

Part Four: What to Expect During the Journey

11. Decisions, Decisions, Decisions
  · The American Pregnancy Association was a helpful resource when looking for healthy habits, dieting, vitamins, and minerals essential to getting pregnant. http://americanpregnancy.org/naturally/get-pregnant-naturally
  · BabyHopes.com was referenced on a few occasions, for herbs that benefit women and for herbs that benefit men. Here are the direct links for each page:
    o http://www.babyhopes.com/articles/herbs.html
    o http://www.babyhopes.com/articles/what-herbs-help-increase-fertility-in-men.html
  · BabyCenter was used in reference to soy isoflavones. https://www.babycenter.com/404_can-soy-isoflavones-help-me-get-pregnant_10364266.bc
  · FertilAid can be found at http://www.fertilaid.com/
  · Fertility Blend can be found at http://www.fertilityblend.com/
  · WebMD was referenced in regard to treatment options available to infertility couples based on what the cause is. The direct link is http://www.webmd.com/infertility-and-reproduction/tc/fertility-problems-treatment-overview
  · To find out more about surrogacy, please visit WebMD's website at http://www.webmd.com/infertility-and-reproduction/guide/using-surrogate-mother
  · I had briefly mentioned my friend would be my surrogate like a character from the show, *Friends*. Here is a website to check out about *Friends*: https://en.wikipedia.org/wiki/Friends

12. What Do I Do Now?
  · To learn more about some of the Biblical examples of waiting that I gave, please see the following:
    o Abraham and Sarah – Genesis 15-18 and 21
    o Jacob – Genesis 28 and 29
    o Israel – Exodus 12-40, all of Leviticus, Numbers, and Deuteronomy, as well as Joshua 1-3
  · To read the entire article, "The Unwelcome Gift of Waiting" by Vaneetha Rendall Risner, please visit http://www.desiringgod.org/articles/the-unwelcome-gift-of-

waiting
- For all the ideas that RESOLVE gave on passing your time while waiting, please check out http://www.resolve.org/support/Managing-Infertility-Stress/grieving-and-growing-creative-outlets-to-grieving-during-infertility.html

13. Testing, Testing, 1, 2, 3
- To learn more about some of the Biblical examples of testing that I gave, please see the following:
  o Abraham – Genesis 22
  o Israel – there are various times when Israel was tested. Their full story is found in the books of Exodus, Leviticus, Numbers, Deuteronomy, and Judges. Of course, their history doesn't stop there, but these books share the testing I referred to
  o Job – the entire book of Job
  o Jesus – Matthew 4
- To read the full article Scary Mommy did on how infertility before parenthood changes you, please visit http://www.scarymommy.com/infertility-before-parenthood-changes-you/

14. No Pain, No Gain
- To learn more about Joni Eareckson Tada and her story, please check out this website: http://www.joniearecksontadastory.com/
- Jesus is the best example of suffering. I highly recommend reading about His birth, life, death, and resurrection in the gospels of Matthew and Luke

Part Five: What to Remember About the Journey

15. Tale as Old as Time
- For a quick reference, here are the women who dealt with infertility in the Bible, as well as where their story is told:
  o Sarah – Genesis 15-18 and 21
  o Rebekah – Genesis 25
  o Rachel – Genesis 29 and 30
  o Manoah's wife – Judges 13
  o Hannah – 1 Samuel 1
  o The woman from Shunem – 2 Kings 4
  o Elizabeth – Luke 1
- Arizona's Center for Fertility Studies has a webpage on infertility's history. I referenced some of it in the book, but to see the complete history, please visit: https://www.acfs2000.com/history_of_infertility.html
- In regard to the history of infertility, here are websites you can check out for further study on the names I listed:
  o Hippocrates – https://en.wikipedia.org/wiki/Hippocrates
  o Galen – https://en.wikipedia.org/wiki/Galen
  o Smellie – https://en.wikipedia.org/wiki/William_Smellie_(obstetrician)

16. Show Business
- Popsugar.com is where I found an article about celebrities who have struggled with infertility. https://www.popsugar.com/moms/Celebrities-Who-Have-Struggled-Infertility-38954694?stream-view=itphto-38956378
- Here are websites for celebrities and shows that I mentioned. They are in the same order as they appeared in the chapter.

o Mariah Carey – http://www.mariahcarey.com/
o Gwen Stefani – https://www.gwenstefani.com/
  § No Doubt – http://www.nodoubt.com/
o Nicole Kidman – http://nicolekidmanofficial.com/
  § Tom Cruise – http://www.tomcruise.com/
  § Keith Urban – http://keithurban.net/
o Courteney Cox – https://en.wikipedia.org/wiki/Courteney_Cox
  § *Friends* – https://en.wikipedia.org/wiki/Friends
  § Matt Lauer – https://en.wikipedia.org/wiki/Matt_Lauer
  § *Dateline NBC* – http://www.nbcnews.com/dateline
  § The actual interview Courteney did with Matt can be found here: http://www.nbcnews.com/id/4907943/ns/dateline-nbc-newsmakers/t/life-imitates-art-courteney-cox
  § Jennifer Aniston – https://en.wikipedia.org/wiki/Jennifer_Aniston
o Kim Kardashian – https://en.wikipedia.org/wiki/Kim_Kardashian
o Jimmy Fallon – https://en.wikipedia.org/wiki/Jimmy_Fallon
o Sarah Jessica Parker – https://en.wikipedia.org/wiki/Sarah_Jessica_Parker
  § Matthew Broderick – https://en.wikipedia.org/wiki/Matthew_Broderick
o Brooke Shields – https://en.wikipedia.org/wiki/Brooke_Shields
o Céline Dion – http://www.celinedion.com/
o Hugh Jackman – https://en.wikipedia.org/wiki/Hugh_Jackman
o Rod Stewart – http://www.rodstewart.com/category/news/
o Giuliana Rancic – http://www.giulianarancic.com/
  § *E! News* – http://www.eonline.com/
o Sherri Shepherd – http://www.sherrishepherd.com/
  § *The View* – http://abc.go.com/shows/the-view

17. Survey Says
· The survey I conducted was done through SurveyMonkey. They make it super easy to create and share surveys. They also do a great job at displaying the results in charts and percentages, making it easy to interpret! https://www.surveymonkey.com/

18. Now Let's Get Real
· I referenced Chris Daughtry. His official website is http://www.daughtryofficial.com/
o His song, "Home," can be watched on YouTube here: https://www.youtube.com/watch?v=7bnX-6sJZBw
· Erin's blog, Living Life with Character, can be found here: http://livinglifewithcharacter.blogspot.com/
· Jennifer mentioned the Huffington Post. Their website is http://www.huffingtonpost.com/
· Linda mentioned *700 Club* and Pat Robertson. Here are their respective websites:
o http://www1.cbn.com/700club
o http://patrobertson.com/
· Lindsey's blog, By Grace the Roberts, can be found here: https://bygracetheroberts.wordpress.com/
o The Stork product from Walgreens that she mentioned can be found here: https://www.storkotc.com/walgreens/
· Sandy's blogs can be found on her website located here: http://www.getpregnantover40.com/
o Her book, *You Can Get Pregnant Over 40, Naturally II*, can be purchased from her website here: http://www.getpregnantover40.com/purchase-online.htm

19. We're All in This Together
   · Here are the direct links to the online forums I would recommend joining:
     o Two Week Wait – http://www.twoweekwait.com/community/
     o RESOLVE – http://www.resolve.org/support/online-support-communities.html
     o JustMommies – http://www.justmommies.com/forums/
   · Here are the direct links to the Facebook groups I would recommend joining:
     o Seeking God Through Infertility & Child Loss –
        https://www.facebook.com/groups/681836385254341/
     o Infertility Support – Christians –
        https://www.facebook.com/groups/1407136412923982/
     o Christian Infertility Support Group –
        https://www.facebook.com/groups/1773912026169828
     o Infertility Issues, Awareness, and Support Group –
        https://www.facebook.com/groups/765136583590428/
     o Infertility, Pregnancy Difficulty, and Miscarriage Support Group –
        https://www.facebook.com/groups/1560497460931253/
   · I mentioned a quote by Dave G. Llewellyn, who runs the Facebook page called Inspire
     Me. The direct link to that is https://www.facebook.com/inspire.me.page/

Part Six: What to Cling to Through the Journey

20. You're My Inspiration
   · The following three websites were used in finding inspirational quotes:
     o https://www.babble.com/pregnancy/20-quotes-to-inspire-your-fertility-journey/
     o https://www.chelseafertilitynyc.com/15-quotes-inspire-journey-parenthood/
     o https://www.brainyquote.com/quotes/topics/topic_inspirational.html
   · Many quotes were given from historical people. Here are their respective websites so
     that you can find out more about them should you wish to:
     o Charles S. Spurgeon – https://en.wikipedia.org/wiki/Charles_Spurgeon
     o Robert Brault – http://quotesabout.us/author/r/robert-brault
     o Norman Vincent Peale – https://en.wikipedia.org/wiki/Norman_Vincent_Peale
     o Winston Churchill – https://en.wikipedia.org/wiki/Winston_Churchill
     o Victor Hugo – https://en.wikipedia.org/wiki/Victor_Hugo
     o Maya Angelou – https://en.wikipedia.org/wiki/Maya_Angelou
     o Louisa May Alcott – https://en.wikipedia.org/wiki/Louisa_May_Alcott
     o Margaret Drabble – https://en.wikipedia.org/wiki/Margaret_Drabble
     o Jimmy Dean – https://en.wikipedia.org/wiki/Jimmy_Dean
     o Theodore Roosevelt – https://en.wikipedia.org/wiki/Theodore_Roosevelt
     o Joseph Campbell – https://en.wikipedia.org/wiki/Joseph_Campbell
     o Audrey Hepburn – https://en.wikipedia.org/wiki/Audrey_Hepburn
     o Francis of Assisi – https://en.wikipedia.org/wiki/Francis_of_Assisi
     o Walt Whitman – https://en.wikipedia.org/wiki/Walt_Whitman
     o Ralph Waldo Emerson – https://en.wikipedia.org/wiki/Ralph_Waldo_Emerson
   · There were four novels I recommended to read. Here are their links on Amazon where
     you can not only read more about them, but purchase should you wish to:
     o *Hannah's Hope* by Jennifer Saake – https://www.amazon.com/dp/B00IDHVV8C
     o *Not Alone* edited by Jessica Snell – https://www.amazon.com/dp/B018UQNHTQ
     o *Plus or Minus* by Matt and Cheri Appling –
        https://www.amazon.com/dp/B00LP1DD2K
     o *Empty Womb* by Marlo Schalesky – https://www.amazon.com/dp/B00B8568G6
   · For each song that I recommended, I am going to give you the performer's website, as

<u>well as a link to a YouTube video:</u>
- o Casting Crowns – https://www.castingcrowns.com
    - § "Praise You in This Storm" Video – https://www.youtube.com/watch?v=vCpP0mFD9F0
- o Kirk Franklin – https://www.facebook.com/KirkFranklin
    - § Toby Mac – http://tobymac.com
    - § "I Am God" Video – https://www.youtube.com/watch?v=XdDoYAygC1Y
- o Bethel – https://www.bethelmusic.com
    - § "It Is Well" Video – https://www.youtube.com/watch?v=YNqo4Un2uZI
- o Kellie Coffey – https://www.kelliecoffey.com
    - § "I Would Die for That" Video – https://www.youtube.com/watch?v=JqfGqOx2iDQ
- o The Afters – http://www.theafters.com
    - § "Light Up the Sky" Video – https://www.youtube.com/watch?v=8LQH6UDi15s
- o Matthew West – https://www.matthewwest.com
    - § "Strong Enough" Video – https://www.youtube.com/watch?v=knuHDPbE5es
- o Robbie Seay Band – https://www.robbieseayband.com
    - § "Song of Hope" Video – https://www.youtube.com/watch?v=w8EndRfdVoc
- o Dixie Chicks – https://www.dixiechicks.com
    - § "So Hard" Video – https://www.youtube.com/watch?v=sBj0ZobEVVA
- o Martina McBride – https://www.martinamcbride.com
    - § "Anyway" Video – https://www.youtube.com/watch?v=6uLtyzRgmyI
- o Plumb – https://www.plumbmusic.net
    - § "Need You Now" Video – https://www.youtube.com/watch?v=9ylnx0NA9X4
- o Miley Cyrus – https://www.mileycyrus.com
    - § "The Climb" Video – https://www.youtube.com/watch?v=NG2zyeVRcbs
- · More information on the movie, *Facing the Giants*, can be found at https://www.facingthegiants.com/
- · I referenced AmateurNester and the prayer exercise that Lisa Newton created. You can find that and so many more helpful resources at http://www.amateurnester.com/

21. This Too Shall Pass
- · The quote I used in this chapter about being okay in the end is a quote I got from Babble.com. As mentioned previously, many other quotes I listed in Chapter 20 were found here as well. The direct webpage from Babble that lists quotes to inspire your infertility journey is, again, https://www.babble.com/pregnancy/20-quotes-to-inspire-your-fertility-journey/

Part Seven: A Final Word

22. Anything Goes
- · Please contact me right away should any information presented in this book be insensitive and/or misrepresented. While I did my best to provide accurate information in a manner that is suitable to those reading it, I am only human. To contact me, please email me at franceshoelsema@gmail.com and/or go to my website at http://franceshoelsema.com/ and fill out the form found on the Contact page. Thank you!

9 798503 574791